The Flavors of Mackinac

This cookbook is a collection of favorite recipes,
which are not necessarily original recipes.

Copyright© Mackinac Island Medical Center
Post Office Box 536
Market Street
Mackinac Island, Michigan 49757
906-847-3582

All rights reserved. No part of this book may be reproduced in
any manner whatsoever without written permission.

Designed, Edited, and Manufactured by
Favorite Recipes® Press
an imprint of

FRP™

P.O. Box 305142, Nashville, Tennessee 37230
1-800-358-0560

Library of Congress Number: 97-72594
ISBN: 0-9658036-0-0

Manufactured in the United States of America
First Printing: 1997   6,000 copies
Second Printing: 2002   6,000 copies

The proceeds from the sale of *The Flavors of Mackinac*
will be donated to Mackinac Island Medical Center.

Preface

In the early 1950s, a group of Mackinac Island residents began a campaign to build a new Island Medical Center. Through the efforts of the community the present Medical Center became a reality.

One of the means of fund raising was a group of Island women who called themselves Grandma's Kitchen. Through bake sales, a significant amount of money was raised. From Grandma's Kitchen and bake sales, Island nurse Stella King got the idea for a cookbook to be created, to raise money for the operation of the Medical Center.

The Mackinac Island Medical Center began seeing patients in early 1954, through the fund-raising efforts of the Mackinac Island community. In the first years of operation the clinic was licensed as a one-bed maternity hospital, and was staffed by one doctor and one nurse, Stella King, R.N. Although the Board of Directors of the Medical Center began recruiting efforts, the Island was basically served by visiting doctors for almost two years.

Through the efforts of the Island's mayor, Margaret Doud, an agreement was signed in 1981 with the Michigan Academy of Family Physicians, who agreed to help staff the Island's Medical Center by sending third-year Family Practice residents to work under the auspices of the Island's year-round physician. In the last fifteen years, several hundred Family Practice Physicians have spent rotations at the Island's Medical Center, working with the year-round doctor.

In the late summer of 1980, two members of the Medical Center's Board of Directors were preparing for a benefit Tag Day to raise funds for the clinic when a director of William Beaumont Hospital Corporation, vacationing on the Island, asked what they were doing. When they explained the difficulty of funding the Medical Center costs, he asked what his group could do to help. As a result of his help, the Medical Center entered into a management contract with Beaumont Hospital Corporation in May of 1981. That contract is still in effect, and has greatly benefited the Medical Center.

The *Historical Mackinac Island Cook Book* has fulfilled the dreams of Grandma's Kitchen. In the past thirty years it has raised over fifty thousand dollars to purchase vital equipment and to keep the building in repair. As this new design and update of the cookbook goes into print, with it go our thanks and admiration for their accomplishments and for a job well done.

Acknowledgements

We would like to thank all the people who contributed so much to this book—in particular all those who donated recipes and organized them, wrote copy, and in anyway contributed support. We would especially like to thank the artists who contributed to this endeavor: Leanne Brodeur, Trish Martin, and Marlee Brown Musser. Trish and Leanne, who contributed the line art, are both lifelong year-round residents and businesswomen of Mackinac Island. Marlee Brown Musser, who donated the beautiful cover art, is a renowned artist.

Marlee was raised in Petoskey, on the shore of Lake Michigan. Her love for nature was fostered there and in the mountains of the United States and Austria, where her ski racing career took her to train and compete as a Junior Olympian, State Champion, and Collegiate All-American.

A graduate of the University of Michigan, Marlee has studied at U. C., Berkeley; En Plein Air School of Painting in Paris, France; the Art Students League of New York; and the National Academy of Design.

Her oil paintings hang in many private and corporate collections in the United States and abroad, most notably in Washington, D. C., at the White House.

She has exhibited extensively, including exhibitions at the Wally Findlay Galleries and the Galerie Chabin in Paris.

Marlee has her own gallery and studio in Harbor Springs. She divides her time between there and her home on Mackinac Island. Her winters are reserved for cultivating her artistic evolution through painting excursions abroad and trips to her New York City studio.

Contents

Introduction, 6

Governor's Mansion, 14

Savory Beginnings, 19
Appetizers
Soups
Salads

Satisfying Main Events, 45
Entrées
Side Dishes

Tasteful Extras, 87
Breads

Sweet Endings, 115
Desserts

Index, 170

Order Information, 175

Introduction

Mackinac Island, at the crossroads of the upper Great Lakes, has been a gathering place for hundreds of years. Native Americans, French, English, and Irish, among others, have been drawn to this island and brought with them their own ways of preparing food. Using what was locally available, through hunting, fishing, and from gardens, and from those things that were imported, islanders created many hardy meals and dishes which are still popular today. This book brings together many of Mackinac's favorite recipes along with a brief history and interesting information about the island in hopes that it can present the true "Flavor of Mackinac."

History

The Island appeared about 11,000 years ago when the Wisconsin Glacier receded. Over the centuries the water levels rose and fell, eroding away steep cliffs and forming unusual rock formations.

The Ojibwa and Ottawa came to the Straits region sometime after 1,100 A.D. According to their oral tradition they journeyed here from the "great salt sea" to the east, and after many hardships they were led to this area rich with wild game, fish, and birds. Wild rice was abundant in the wetlands, and the forests were rich with maple trees for sugaring. And to further show that this was the area where they were meant to dwell, there was an island that had been blessed by the spirits with rock archways, altars, and outcroppings.

The first Europeans to pass through the Straits of Mackinac were the early French explorers, including Nicolet and LaSalle, who in the 1600s were searching the Great Lakes for the legendary Northwest Passage to China. In 1669, Father Jacques Marquette and Father Claude Dablon, French Jesuits, canoed to the Straits to establish a mission. It was first established on the island but a year later was moved to present

day St. Ignace, in Michigan's upper peninsula. Around this small mission a French fort was established to protect the expanding fur trade. This outpost was eventually abandoned by the French only to be reestablished in 1715 on the south side of the Straits at Fort Michilimackinac, near present-day Mackinaw City. This small palisaded village was a vital link in the extremely profitable fur trade.

    In the 1750s war broke out between the French and the English, and by 1761 the British flag flew over the walls of Michilimackinac. Generally speaking, the French inhabitants remained and continued working in the fur trade, though now for the British. Many of them had intermarried with the Ottawa and Ojibwa and were a permanent part of the region. These people of mixed blood were usually referred to as the "métis" and were the backbone of the fur trade.

    The British remained at Fort Michilimackinac until the Revolutionary War, when the commanding officer moved his garrison to the more defensible heights of Mackinac Island in 1780, thus establishing the first permanent settlement on Mackinac Island.

    In 1796 the first American troops marched into Fort Mackinac, however they did not hold it for long. War with Britain again broke out in 1812. The English troops at Fort St. Joseph had word of the declaration of war before the Americans at nearby Mackinac. On June 17th, under the cover of darkness, a large contingent of British troops and native allies landed on the north end of Mackinac and dragged a cannon to the heights behind the fort. As the sun rose, a single cannon shot broke the stillness, rousing the unsuspecting American soldiers. As the American garrison was not only unprepared but also greatly outnumbered, they immediately surrendered the fort to the British, thus ending the first conflict of the war. Several times during the next few years the Americans attempted to recapture the Island, however, it was not until the peace treaty was signed that the Americans troops returned to Mackinac.

During the years immediately following the war the fur trade expanded. John Jacob Astor's American Fur Company established its headquarters on Mackinac. Millions of dollars worth of furs were brought to the island, baled, and shipped back East. In the 1830s the fur trade began to decline due to a decrease in the number of fur-bearing animals in the region and a reduction in demand.

The fishing industry expanded as the fur trade failed. Many Irish immigrants came to the area in the mid-eighteen hundreds to escape the potato famine in Ireland, and fishing became their mainstay and that of the island. Mackinac became the largest distributor of whitefish and lake trout on the Great Lakes during the mid-nineteenth century, with enough business to keep numerous coopers busy making barrels in which to store and ship the fish. Special fishing boats, known as Mackinac boats, were designed for these inland seas. These sturdy craft had two masts and a jib and were pointed at both bow and stern.

After the Civil War, tourism became the new industry at Mackinac. As the industrial revolution expanded, cities grew throughout the Midwest. A new prosperity brought with it more leisure time, and visitors flocked to this island to escape the noise and heat of the cities and the hay fever of the farms. It took only a day or so to reach Mackinac by steamer or train from Chicago, Detroit, or Cleveland.

In 1875, the Federal government created the second national park in the United States, Mackinac National Park, to preserve the natural beauty of the island and its historic buildings. By the 1880s, Mackinac was the most fashionable resort in the Midwest. Summer cottages were being built on both private property and on land leased for the Park on the East and West Bluffs of the island. At about the same

time, plans were underway to build Mackinac's premiere hotel. Several railway companies and the Detroit and Cleveland Navigation Company joined to create the Mackinac Island Hotel Company. In 1887, they constructed the spectacular Greek-revival-styled hotel originally known as Plank's Grand Hotel. It soon became simply the Grand Hotel. And "grand" it was and is. Its porch, approximately 627 feet long, is one of the longest in the world. People such as the Potter Palmers, Marshall Fields, the Swifts and Armours of Chicago, as well as Adolphus Bush, brewer of St. Louis, and lumber barons like the Blodgetts and Algers, began to stay at the hotel.

In 1895, Mackinac National Park became the Mackinac Island State Park, the first state park in Michigan. Three years later a momentous occurrence took place on Mackinac which would shape the history of the island. In 1898, an ordinance was passed prohibiting motorized vehicles on Mackinac Island. Horses and bicycles were to be the mode of transportation.

Today

Tourism continues to be the lifeblood of Mackinac. Yearly the island welcomes hundreds of thousands of visitors to its peaceful shores. They come for the same reasons the visitors came a hundred years ago and for the most part they still come by ferry boats. The Arnold Line, Sheplers and Starline boat companies bring passengers, freight, mail, food, and everything else needed to support a thriving community. Motorized vehicles (with the exception of emergency and maintenance vehicles) are still banned on the island, so bicycles, horses, and horse-drawn carriages continue to be the major forms of transportation. In fact, the Mackinac Island Carriage Tours boast the largest livery stable in the world.

Fort Mackinac, the fort built during the American Revolution, is open daily with guided tours and demonstrations, along with a half dozen other historic buildings. About 80 percent of the island is still state park with wooded paths and wonderful rock formations. There are numerous gift shops, restaurants, hotels, and B.& B.s throughout the town which welcome visitors from May through October.

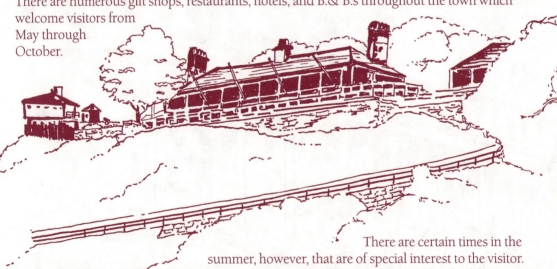

There are certain times in the summer, however, that are of special interest to the visitor. In the first couple of weeks of June, Mackinac Island celebrates its Lilac Festival. Mackinac has one of the widest assortments and some of the oldest and largest lilacs in the country. Many of the trees are 150 to 200 years old. In 1947, resident nurse Stella King began the festival, which has now greatly expanded to include one of the largest festival parades in Michigan and the only one that can boast entirely horse-drawn floats!

Another exciting time is when the Yacht Races hit the island during the last two weeks of July. For about a hundred years, sailboats have raced hundreds of miles up Lakes Michigan and Huron in the Chicago or Port Huron to Mackinac Races. Today, over 300 boats enter each race and it is a beautiful sight when they make their way to the island with their colorful spinnakers and bloopers unfurled.

As the fall draws to a close and fewer and fewer visitors come to the island, Mackinac becomes a quieter place. Most of the 500 horses are loaded onto freight boats and are sent to farms off island for the winter. More and more of the people coming off the boats are workmen dressed in their tan Carharts heading for the next construction or reconstruction job. Summer cottages on the East and West Bluffs are closed and fewer and fewer shops are open. This is the time for storms. When the winds howl along at 50 or 60 miles per hour, the waves run high, and the rain or snow beats down. This might sound kind of bleak, but the islanders look forward to this time when life slows down and we are no longer working 50-, 60-, or 70-hour weeks. Besides having more time to enjoy the island, locals also get a chance to visit with one another. Islanders often claim that they say goodby to their year-round friends in the spring and greet them again in the fall.

November brings with it hunting season. Hunting has been a tradition at Mackinac even long after its necessity has passed. Early accounts of the region refer to the abundance of game and wild fowl. Today most people hunt rabbit, fowl, and of course deer (in this book you can find several recipes for venison, often served with traditional gleasants, French dumplings). There is no hunting permitted on the island so on crisp fall days locals can be seen clad in hunting gear loading their supplies into small aluminum boats to descend on their preferred hunting camp on neighboring islands, not unlike their ancestors loading their birch-bark canoes.

One of the first big events of the "off" season is the Christmas Bazaar. This is held every year on the first weekend in December, though preparations begin long before. Ste. Anne's Catholic Church, the Mackinac Island Medical Center, and Trinity Episcopal Church all get together to put on this event. Booths are set up with hand-knitted and crochet items, baked goods, Christmas decorations and plants, and items donated from some of our island shops. Wonderful dinners and snacks are prepared and sold, along with raffles for everything from dolls to snowmobiles. There are activities for the kids, and Santa arrives not on one of our

sleighs (which are commonly seen on the island) but on the motorized fire engine. One of the main events of the bazaar is the auction. The items auctioned include everything from dinners at the Grand Hotel to handmade quilts and Pistons tickets, from homemade ornaments to a cruise on a Great Lakes freighter. During the bazaar, the city Christmas tree is set up in the middle of the main street of the island. Christmas songs and carols are sung somewhat in tune and finally the switch is thrown and the tree lights up, officially opening the holiday season.

Christmas is a special time at Mackinac. Many family members return to the island. People take snowmobile rides to look at the Christmas lights in the village and town and to see the Fort lit up. Even the ferries get into the act with colored lights strung along the rails of the boat and Christmas carols played over the public address system at the dock. Almost everyone goes to the Christmas program put on by the schoolchildren. All three of the churches which are open in the winter have services, but one that is especially looked forward to is the one at Ste. Anne's. This is because after the mass everyone gets together to eat St. Fanny cake and the wonderful meat pies that have been made by the ladies of the island (you can find the recipes in this book).

After Christmas is New Years. It used to be that the New Years celebration on the island was a local event with parties put on by the Fire Department at the Community Hall, at the Mustang Lounge, and in family homes. These days visitors have discovered winter at Mackinac and are coming in numbers to enjoy the cross country skiing, sleigh rides, and to see in the New Year.

When winter's still, cold days hit and the boats have stopped running, the ice finally "makes" (freezes). Islanders can then cross to the mainland on the "ice bridge." In years past, dogsleds and horse-drawn sleighs would cross the ice to bring mail and supplies. Today, snowmobiles ply the ice in a steady stream, guided by the islanders' discarded Christmas trees which mark the safest route over the thickest ice. Somedays the bridge is so busy that it is laughingly referred to as I-75 extended. Great Lakes Air also supplies

transportation to the island. In short, breathtaking flights from Mackinac County Airport in St. Ignace, planes bring passengers, freight, and the mail.

Winter Festival comes about a month after the New Years visitors have left. This event is held on the first weekend in February and is sponsored by the Mackinac Island Recreational Development Inc. or M.I.R.D. (this group has taken the old gravel pit on the island and turned it into Turtle Park). People come to enjoy the weekend activities, which include the blindfold snowmobile race, snow volleyball, a silent auction, a Gourmet Glide (or, as it is laughingly called, the Glide and Graze), a wonderful brunch, and, most importantly, the opportunity to vote for the pictures which will appear in the Mackinac Island calendar, the Seasons of Mackinac.

March can sometimes seem like the longest month of the year. Winter has been going on for what seems like forever, the ice bridge may or may not be good, and it is still at least a month before the boats begin to run. One thing that helps us to survive the doldrums of March is St. Patrick's Day. The Mustang Lounge usually has several days in which Hilt Frazer puts together a pickup band of locals, in addition to his family, and the bar swings with Irish songs and local favorites. The church puts on a big dinner for everyone with door prizes, and a raffle with a $5,000 prize. People also have smaller parties in their homes. Any excuse for a get-together in March is a good one.

All too soon the winter is gone, the snow melts, and the boats begin to run. The first boat of the year signals the beginning of the busy season. Workers and horses begin to return, supplies are brought in, and everyone hurries to get ready for a new summer season. The game nights and parties of the winter are but a memory, but everyone knows that come November we'll see our winter friends again and have time to enjoy each other and our island home.

Governor's Mansion

As visitors approach Mackinac, they are greeted with a view of some of the island's magnificent summer cottages that dot the East and West Bluffs. One such cottage, standing like a sentinel on guard near Fort Mackinac, is now known as the Governor's Mansion. This stately mansion was built for Lawrence Young, in 1901, by local carpenter Patrick Doud and a crew of seventy-five islanders at a cost of $15,000. In 1944, when the owner had fallen on hard times, the State of Michigan purchased the house for its building price and it became the official summer residence of the Governor of Michigan. This stately home, with its panoramic view of the Straits, has been the host to many notable guests including Presidents Gerald Ford, Bill Clinton, and John F. Kennedy.

Our present governor and his family utilize the house for much of the summer and graciously open it to the public for tours every Wednesday morning from June 15 until Labor Day. Among the many roles provided by a governor and family is that of entertaining at formal dinners for constituents and visiting dignitaries. Menus are an important consideration for such events. Here, Michigan First Lady Michelle Engler and several preceding First Ladies share with you their favorite recipes.

Cheese Enchiladas

1/4 to 1/2 cup chili powder
2 to 3 tablespoons vegetable oil
1 teaspoon salt
2 (15-ounce) cans tomato sauce   1/2 cup water
16 ounces (or more) Monterey Jack cheese, grated,
or queso fresco ranchero, crumbled
1 medium onion, finely chopped
1/2 cup vegetable oil
20 red or plain corn tortillas

Heat the chili powder and 2 to 3 tablespoons vegetable oil in a large skillet over low heat for 3 to 4 minutes. Add the salt and tomato sauce. Simmer for 10 to 15 minutes. Stir in the water. Mix the cheese and onion in a bowl. Heat 1/2 cup vegetable oil in a small skillet. Dip 1 tortilla quickly in a shallow dish filled with lukewarm water, then in the heated vegetable oil and finally in the chili sauce. Spoon about 2 tablespoons of the cheese mixture onto the tortilla and roll up. Place in a 9x13-inch baking dish. Repeat the process with the remaining tortillas. Spoon any remaining chili sauce over the enchiladas and sprinkle with the remaining cheese mixture. Bake at 400 degrees for 15 minutes.
May prepare the enchiladas and chill, covered with plastic wrap, until ready to serve, letting the enchiladas come to room temperature before baking.
Yield: 10 servings

First Lady Michelle Engler

Party Chicken

4 chicken breasts, boned and split
3 tablespoons butter
Salt and pepper to taste
2 (16-ounce) cans small potatoes, drained
1 cup cubed cooked ham
1 (4-ounce) can mushrooms, drained
2 tablespoons flour
2 cups cream   1/2 cup white wine
1 (16-ounce) can white grapes, drained

Rinse the chicken and pat dry. Brown the chicken in the butter in a skillet. Season with salt and pepper. Place the chicken in a buttered baking dish. Add the potatoes to the skillet. Cook until brown. Stir in the ham and mushrooms. Arrange the potato mixture around the chicken. Blend the flour into the pan drippings in the skillet. Stir in the cream and wine gradually. Cook until smooth and thickened, stirring constantly. Pour over the chicken. Bake, covered, at 350 degrees for 50 minutes. Add the grapes. Bake for 10 minutes longer. Serve with a grapefruit and orange salad.
Yield: 8 servings

First Lady Helen Milliken

Asparagus and Tomato Casserole

1/4 cup chopped celery
1 tablespoon chopped green bell pepper
2 tablespoons vegetable oil
1 (20-ounce) can tomatoes
2 tablespoons sugar
2 tablespoons cornstarch   2 tablespoons water
1 (10-ounce) package frozen chopped asparagus
1/2 cup cubed Cheddar cheese
1/2 teaspoon dillseeds   Seasoned salt to taste
1/2 cup cracker crumbs
1 tablespoon melted butter

Cook the celery and green pepper in the vegetable oil in a skillet for 5 minutes. Add the tomatoes, sugar, cornstarch and water. Cook until thickened, stirring constantly. Cook the asparagus using the package directions and drain. Arrange in a buttered baking dish. Add the tomato sauce. Sprinkle with the cheese, dillseeds and seasoned salt. Cover the top with a mixture of cracker crumbs and butter. Bake at 350 degrees or until golden brown.
Yield: 4 to 6 servings

First Lady Lenore Romney

Cheesecake Cookies

5 tablespoons butter, softened
1/3 cup packed brown sugar
1 cup flour   1/4 cup chopped walnuts
1/2 cup sugar   8 ounces cream cheese, softened
1 egg   2 tablespoons milk
1 tablespoon lemon juice   1/2 teaspoon vanilla extract

Cream the butter and brown sugar in a mixer bowl until light and fluffy. Add the flour and walnuts and mix well. Reserve 1 cup of the mixture for the topping. Press the remaining mixture in an 8x8-inch nonstick baking pan. Bake at 350 degrees for 12 to 15 minutes. Beat the sugar and cream cheese in a mixer bowl until smooth. Add the egg, milk, lemon juice and vanilla and beat well. Spread in the prepared pan. Sprinkle with the reserved mixture. Bake for 25 minutes. Let stand until cool. Chill in the refrigerator. Cut into triangles just before serving.
Yield: 16 servings

First Lady Paula L. Blanchard

Surprise Walnut Pie

3 egg whites   1 cup sugar
1/4 teaspoon cream of tartar
1/2 teaspoon vanilla extract   1/4 teaspoon salt
12 saltine crackers, coarsely chopped
1 cup chopped walnuts   Whipped cream

Beat the egg whites in a mixer bowl until foamy. Add sugar and cream of tartar gradually, beating until stiff peaks form. Beat in the vanilla and salt. Fold in the crackers and 2/3 cup of the walnuts. Spoon into a greased and lightly floured pie plate. Bake at 325 degrees for 45 minutes. Let stand until cool. Spread whipped cream over the top. Sprinkle with the remaining 1/3 cup walnuts.
Yield: 8 servings

First Lady Nancy Williams

Savory Beginnings

Appetizers, Soups, & Salads

Boursin Cheese

1 clove of garlic, crushed
1 cup whipped butter
16 ounces cream cheese, softened
1/2 teaspoon salt
1/2 teaspoon basil
1/2 teaspoon marjoram
1/2 teaspoon chives
1 teaspoon dillweed
1 tablespoon chopped fresh parsley
1/4 teaspoon freshly ground pepper

Combine the garlic, butter, cream cheese, salt, basil, marjoram, chives, dillweed, parsley and pepper in a food processor container. Process until smooth. Serve on assorted crackers, melba toast or bagels. *Yield: 20 to 25 servings.*

Stephanie and Andrew McGreevy

Cheese Ball

2 (5-ounce) jars Old English cheese spread
4 ounces bleu cheese
8 ounces cream cheese, softened
1 onion, grated
1 tablespoon Worcestershire sauce
1 (3-ounce) package pecans, chopped
Chopped parsley

Combine the cheese spread, bleu cheese, cream cheese, onion and Worcestershire sauce in a mixer bowl and mix well. Stir in the pecans. Shape into a ball and cover with the parsley. Chill, wrapped in plastic wrap, in the refrigerator. *Yield: 20 to 25 servings.*

Theta Paetschow

Herb Cheese Spread

1 clove of garlic
¼ teaspoon salt
12 ounces cream cheese, softened
8 ounces feta cheese
½ cup mayonnaise
¼ teaspoon basil
¼ teaspoon thyme
¼ teaspoon marjoram
¼ teaspoon oregano
¼ teaspoon dillweed

Press the garlic through a garlic press. Combine the pressed garlic with the salt in a bowl. Combine with the cream cheese, feta cheese, mayonnaise, basil, thyme, marjoram, oregano and dillweed in a food processor or blender container and process until smooth. Spoon into a serving bowl. Chill, covered, for several hours to overnight. Let stand at room temperature for 1 hour before serving. Serve with crackers or hearty bread.
Yield: 20 to 25 servings.

Mary Jane Barnwell

Hot Cheese Dip

2 onions, chopped
¼ cup butter
16 ounces Velveeta cheese, chopped
1 (16-ounce) can tomatoes
2 hot peppers, seeded, chopped
1 tablespoon Worcestershire sauce
Tabasco sauce to taste
Garlic salt to taste (optional)

Brown the onions in the butter in a skillet. Add the cheese. Heat until melted, stirring constantly. Stir in the tomatoes, peppers, Worcestershire sauce, Tabasco sauce and garlic salt. Spoon into a chafing dish. *Yield: 20 to 25 servings.*

Joanne Zwolinski

Triple Cheese Dip

4 ounces cream cheese, softened
2 ounces Cheddar cheese spread, softened
1 cup sour cream

1 ounce Roquefort cheese or bleu cheese, softened
1/2 teaspoon Worcestershire sauce
1/8 teaspoon Tabasco sauce (optional)

1/2 teaspoon seasoned salt
1/4 teaspoon onion powder
Parsley to taste
Dillseeds to taste

Combine the cream cheese, Cheddar cheese spread, 2 tablespoons of the sour cream and Roquefort cheese in a small mixer bowl. Beat at low speed until blended. Add the remaining sour cream, Worcestershire sauce, Tabasco sauce, seasoned salt, onion powder, parsley and dillseeds. Beat at high speed until light and fluffy. Spoon into a serving bowl. Chill, covered, for several hours. Sprinkle with additional parsley, dillseeds and seasoned salt just before serving. May stir in a small amount of milk or coffee cream if the dip becomes too thick. *Yield: 15 to 20 servings.*

Marie Newell

Dill Dip

2/3 cup mayonnaise
2/3 cup sour cream

1 tablespoon parsley flakes
1 teaspoon dillweed

1 teaspoon seasoned salt
1/2 teaspoon garlic salt

Combine the mayonnaise, sour cream, parsley flakes, dillweed, seasoned salt and garlic salt in a bowl and mix well. Spoon into a serving bowl. Chill, covered, overnight. Serve with fresh vegetables for dipping. *Yield: 10 to 15 servings.*

Mary Dufina

Skinny Dipping

2/3 cup mayonnaise
1 tablespoon chopped onion

2/3 cup sour cream
2 1/4 teaspoons dillweed

1 tablespoon Beau Monde seasoning

Mix the mayonnaise, onion, sour cream and seasonings in a bowl. Spoon into a serving bowl. Chill, covered, until serving time. Serve with baby carrots, celery sticks, mushrooms, zucchini, bell peppers and cauliflowerets. *Yield: 10 to 15 servings.*

Kathy Andress

Hot Nacho Dip

1 (8-ounce) can refried beans
1 small bunch green onions or scallions, thinly sliced

1 cup sour cream
1 cup mild or medium chunky salsa
12 ounces Colby cheese or mozzarella cheese, shredded

1 (8-ounce) can sliced black olives, drained (optional)

Spread the refried beans in a 6x10-inch glass baking dish sprayed with nonstick cooking spray. Layer the green onions, sour cream, salsa and cheese over the refried beans. Bake at 325 degrees for 30 to 40 minutes or until bubbly. Sprinkle the olives over the top. Serve with tortilla chips. *Yield: 15 to 20 servings.*

Linda D. Horn

Taco Dip

1 (16-ounce) can refried beans
1 cup mashed avocado
1 cup sour cream
½ cup mayonnaise
2 envelopes taco seasoning mix
1 cup shredded cheese
1 medium onion, chopped
Shredded lettuce
Chopped tomatoes

Spread the refried beans in a 9x13-inch dish. Combine the avocado and sour cream in a bowl and mix well. Spread the avocado mixture over the refried beans. Mix the mayonnaise with the taco seasoning mix in a bowl. Spread over the avocado mixture. Layer the cheese, onion, lettuce and tomatoes over the layers. Serve with corn chips.
Yield: 15 to 20 servings.

Louann Mosley

Liptauer Spread

3 ounces cream cheese, softened
½ cup butter, softened
1 small can rolled anchovies, chopped
2 tablespoons prepared mustard
1 tablespoon minced onion or onion salt
1 teaspoon paprika

Beat the cream cheese and butter in a mixer bowl until light and fluffy. Add the anchovies, mustard, onion and paprika and mix well. Spoon into a serving bowl. Chill, covered, until 1 hour before serving time. *Yield: 15 to 20 servings.*

Kathleen Hoppenrath

Liver Sausage Spread

16 ounces smoked liver sausage
8 ounces cream cheese, softened
¼ cup chopped dill pickles
1 teaspoon Worcestershire sauce
2 tablespoons pickle juice
¼ cup mayonnaise
¼ cup grated onion
¼ teaspoon garlic salt

Combine the sausage, half the cream cheese, pickles, Worcestershire sauce, pickle juice, mayonnaise, onion and garlic salt in a bowl and mix well. Shape the mixture into a log. Chill in the refrigerator. Frost the top of the log with the remaining cream cheese. *Yield: 15 to 20 servings.*

Mary Dufina

Salmon Log

1 (15-ounce) can salmon, drained, flaked
8 ounces cream cheese, softened
1 teaspoon lemon juice
2 teaspoons grated onion
1 teaspoon prepared horseradish
¼ teaspoon salt
¼ teaspoon liquid smoke
Finely chopped pecans
Finely chopped fresh parsley

Combine the salmon, cream cheese, lemon juice, onion, horseradish, salt and liquid smoke in a bowl and mix well. Shape into a log. Roll in pecans and parsley. Chill, wrapped in plastic wrap, overnight. Serve with assorted crackers. *Yield: 15 to 20 servings.*

Janice Lowell

Asparagus Roll-Ups

1 (10-ounce) package frozen asparagus spears
20 slices thin white bread, crusts trimmed

8 ounces cream cheese, softened
1 egg

3 ounces freshly grated Parmesan cheese
1 cup melted butter

Cook the asparagus using the package directions and drain. Flatten each bread slice with a rolling pin. Beat the cream cheese, egg and Parmesan cheese in a mixer bowl until smooth. Spread on each bread slice. Arrange 1 asparagus spear on each bread slice and roll up tightly. Secure with wooden picks if needed. Dip each roll into the melted butter and cut into halves. Place on a baking sheet. Bake at 350 degrees for 15 minutes. May substitute Neufchâtel cheese for the cream cheese and crumbled bleu cheese for the Parmesan cheese. May freeze the roll-ups and thaw the amount needed before slicing and baking. *Yield: 40 servings.*

Lornie Porter

Broccoli and Cheese Skins

1 pound broccoli, finely chopped
1/2 cup chopped mushrooms
1/2 cup minced onion
1 clove of garlic, crushed
2 tablespoons butter
2 cups cooked brown rice

1/4 cup sour cream
2 eggs, beaten
1 cup packed finely grated Cheddar cheese
2 tablespoons chopped parsley
2 tablespoons soy sauce
1/4 teaspoon seasoned salt

Pepper to taste
1/8 teaspoon nutmeg
10 large potato skins, lightly crisped
Grated Cheddar cheese
Paprika to taste
Sunflower seed kernels to taste

Steam the broccoli in a small amount of water in a saucepan just until tender and drain. Sauté the mushrooms, onion and garlic in the butter in a large skillet until tender. Stir in the broccoli. Stir-fry for 1 minute and remove skillet from heat. Stir in the rice. Add the sour cream, eggs, 1 cup Cheddar cheese, parsley, soy sauce, seasoned salt, pepper and nutmeg. Stuff the potato skins with the broccoli mixture. Place on a buttered baking sheet. Sprinkle each potato skin with grated Cheddar cheese, paprika and sunflower seed kernels. Bake at 350 degrees, covered loosely with foil, for 15 to 20 minutes. Uncover and bake for 5 minutes longer. Serve hot. *Yield: 10 servings.*

Melinda Porter

Ham Rolls

Albert and Jane Maury Maverick's ham rolls have been a favorite in San Antonio, Texas, for 100 years. The recipe originated during the post-Civil War days at Piedmont, the hospitable Maury family home in Charlottesville, Virginia, when Virginia ham and other food were scarce. We enjoyed this treat in the 1940s and 1950s at great-grandmother's home on Sunshine Ranch where as many as 150 illustrious guests, children, grandchildren, and great-grandchilden would gather for traditional Sunday suppers.

24 finger rolls	2 tablespoons prepared mustard	1/4 cup pickle juice
1 pound cooked ham	1/4 cup finely chopped celery	6 tablespoons melted butter
1 or 2 sour pickles		

Lay each roll flat on a cutting board and cut off each end with a serrated knife. Cut the rolls into halves and stand each half upright on the trimmed end. Scoop out the centers of the rolls with a small sharp knife or grapefruit spoon to form a shell. Crumble the roll centers onto a baking sheet. Bake at 350 degrees until the crumbs are toasted. Measure 3/4 cup of the crumbs and set aside.

Grind the ham in a food grinder; measure and reserve 3 cups. Grind the pickles in a food grinder; measure and reserve 1/4 cup. Put the reserved bread crumbs through the grinder to absorb any remaining juice. Combine the ham, pickles and bread crumbs in a bowl. Add the mustard, celery and pickle juice and toss well. Dip the edge of each roll shell in the melted butter; spoon a few drops of butter into each shell. Fill the shells with the ham mixture. Arrange the filled rolls in a 9x13-inch baking dish. Bake at 350 degrees for 20 minutes or until brown and heated through. *Yield: 48 servings.*

Amelia Maverick Epler Musser and Margaret Stewart Musser

Cheese Fingers

1 cup butter, softened
8 ounces Cheddar cheese

1 cup whipping cream

1 loaf unsliced
sandwich bread

Melt the butter and cheese in a double boiler. Whip the cream until creamy. Stir into the cheese mixture. Trim and discard crusts from the bread. Cut into 1x1 1/2-inch pieces the width of the bread. Dip into the cheese mixture. Arrange on a baking sheet. Let stand for 4 hours. Bake at 375 degrees for 10 minutes, turning 4 times. *Yield: 36 to 48 servings.*

Mary Miller

Party Mix

1 (7-ounce) package
Cheerios
1 (6-ounce) package rice
Chex
1 (12-ounce) package
wheat Chex

1 (5 3/4-ounce) package
pretzel sticks
1 cup vegetable oil
1/2 cup margarine
1 tablespoon
Worcestershire sauce

1/2 teaspoon Tabasco
sauce
2 tablespoons celery salt
1 tablespoon garlic salt

Mix the cereal and pretzel sticks in a large roasting pan. Combine the vegetable oil, margarine, Worcestershire sauce, Tabasco sauce, celery salt and garlic salt in a small saucepan. Heat until the margarine melts, stirring occasionally. Pour over the cereal mixture and mix well. Bake at 250 degrees for 1 1/2 hours, stirring occasionally. May add peanuts or other kinds of nuts. *Yield: 15 to 20 servings.*

Patrick Chambers

Romanola

4 cups rolled oats
1 cup wheat germ
1/2 cup sesame seeds
1/2 cup sunflower seed kernels
1/2 cup whole wheat flour
1/2 cup chopped nuts
1/2 cup shredded coconut
3/4 cup vegetable oil
3/4 cup honey
2 teaspoons vanilla extract

Combine the oats, wheat germ, sesame seeds, sunflower seed kernels, whole wheat flour, nuts and coconut in a large bowl and mix well. Heat the vegetable oil, honey and vanilla in a saucepan over low heat until warm; do not boil. Pour over the dry ingredients and mix well. Spread on a lightly greased baking sheet. Bake at 200 degrees for 3 to 4 hours, stirring gently every 30 minutes. Let stand overnight to dry. May add raisins or other dried fruit. *Yield: 10 to 15 servings.*

Mary Jane Barnwell

Frozen Daiquiris

1 (3-ounce) can frozen lemonade concentrate
1 lemonade can water
2 lemonade cans rum
14 ounces 7-Up

Combine the lemonade concentrate, water, rum and 7-Up in a freezer-safe container and mix well. Freeze, covered, for 24 hours or longer. Stir before serving. May use a 6-ounce can of frozen lemonade concentrate and increase the amount of 7-Up used. *Yield: 6 to 8 servings.*

Barbara McIntyre

Mackinac Frozen Margaritas

1 (12-ounce) can frozen limeade concentrate
3 limeade cans water
1/2 cup Triple Sec
12 ounces tequila

Mix the limeade concentrate, water, Triple Sec and tequila in a plastic pitcher. Freeze for 4 hours or until slushy. *Yield: 10 to 15 servings.*

Gracie Koerbel

Bean Soup

1 pound dried beans
1 smoked meaty ham bone

3 medium potatoes, peeled, quartered

1 cup chopped celery
1 cup chopped onion
2 cloves of garlic, minced

Rinse and sort the beans. Soak in water to cover in a saucepan overnight and drain. Add enough water to beans to equal 5 pints. Add the ham bone. Simmer for 2 hours or until the beans are very soft. Cook the potatoes in water to cover in a saucepan until tender. Drain and mash the potatoes. Add the mashed potatoes, celery, onion and garlic to the beans. Simmer for 1 hour. Remove the meaty ham bone to a plate. Remove the ham from the bone and discard the bone. Return the ham to the soup. Add salt to taste. Ladle into soup bowls. Yield: 4$^1/_2$ quarts.

Leila Walker

Cucumber Soup

2 large cucumbers
1 teaspoon salt

1 teaspoon cinnamon

1 quart buttermilk
Chopped fresh mint

Peel the cucumbers and cut vertically into quarters. Remove the seeds and chop the cucumbers. Combine the cucumbers, salt and cinnamon in a large bowl and mix well. Stir in the buttermilk. Chill in the refrigerator until icy cold. Ladle into soup bowls and sprinkle with mint. *Yield: 4 servings.*

Janey Hart

Corn Chowder

1/4 cup salt pork, chopped
2 onions, minced
1/2 cup water
2 potatoes, peeled, chopped
1 (16-ounce) can whole kernel corn
2 cups milk
1 teaspoon salt
1/8 teaspoon pepper

Fry the pork in a skillet until nearly crisp. Add the onions. Cook until the onions are golden brown. Add the water and potatoes. Simmer for 5 minutes. Add the corn. Cook for 5 minutes. Stir in the milk, salt and pepper. Simmer until heated through. Ladle into soup bowls. *Yield: 4 servings.*

Stella King

French Canadian Pea Soup

1 (16-ounce) package yellow peas
1 teaspoon baking soda
8 ounces salt pork
2 ribs celery, finely chopped
1 large onion, finely chopped
Salt to taste

Rinse and sort the peas. Place in a saucepan with water to cover. Bring to a boil. Add the baking soda. Boil for 1 minute. Drain and rinse gently. Return the peas to a saucepan with fresh water to cover. Add the salt pork. Bring to a boil. Boil for 2 1/2 hours. Add the celery, onion and salt to taste. Boil for 1 1/2 hours longer, adding additional water as needed for desired consistency. Ladle into soup bowls. May store in the refrigerator but discard the salt pork. *Yield: 4 to 6 servings.*

Nan Rudolph

Carriage House Special German Potato Soup

1 large onion, chopped
2 cups chopped celery
8 medium large potatoes, chopped
2 tablespoons grated carrot

½ cup butter
½ cup flour
3 cups milk
Salt and pepper to taste
3 hard-cooked eggs, coarsely chopped

1 tablespoon chopped parsley
1 tablespoon chopped pimento

Cook the onion and celery in a nonstick skillet until tender. Combine with the potatoes and carrot in a large saucepan. Add enough water to cover. Cook until the potatoes are tender. Melt the butter in a saucepan over low heat. Stir in the flour. Add the milk, stirring constantly. Cook until thickened, stirring constantly. Add to the vegetables. Season with salt and pepper. Stir in the eggs, parsley and pimento. Ladle into soup bowls.
Yield: 4 to 6 servings.

Helen Lynch

Cheesy Vegetable Soup

3 potatoes, peeled, chopped
2 carrots, scraped, sliced
1 small onion, chopped

1 cup chopped broccoli
1 cup chopped cauliflower
2 (10-ounce) cans cream of chicken soup

2 pounds Velveeta cheese, chopped
1 tablespoon parsley flakes

Combine the potatoes, carrots, onion, broccoli and cauliflower with water to cover in a saucepan. Cook until the carrots are tender. Add the canned soup and cheese. Cook until the cheese is melted, stirring constantly. Stir in the parsley flakes. Ladle into soup bowls.
Yield: 6 servings.

Chad Davis

Crab Bisque

1 (4-ounce) can crab meat
1 (10-ounce) can cream of asparagus soup
1 (10-ounce) can cream of mushroom soup
1 (4-ounce) can sliced mushrooms
1 cup cream or half-and-half
1 cup milk
Onion flakes to taste
1/4 cup cooking sherry (optional)
Butter to taste
Paprika to taste
Sprigs of parsley

Combine the crab meat, asparagus soup, mushroom soup, mushrooms, cream, milk, onion flakes and cooking sherry in a saucepan and mix well. Cook over low heat until heated through, stirring constantly to prevent scorching. Ladle into soup bowls. Place a dab of butter in the center of each serving and sprinkle with paprika. Top with a parsley sprig. *Yield: 6 to 8 servings.*

Meg Brown

Fish Chowder

4 ounces salt pork
2 onions, minced
1 rib celery, minced
1 pound fresh firm fish
1 (20-ounce) can tomatoes
2 cups water
1/2 teaspoon thyme
3 medium potatoes, chopped
Salt and pepper to taste
1 teaspoon MSG

Fry the salt pork in a saucepan until crisp. Add the onions and celery. Sauté until the vegetables are tender and golden brown. Add the fish, tomatoes, water, thyme, potatoes, salt, pepper and MSG. Cook gently until the potatoes are tender and the fish flakes easily. Ladle into soup bowls. *Yield: 4 servings.*

Stella King

Apricot Fluff

1 (20-ounce) can crushed pineapple
1 (6-ounce) package apricot gelatin
6 tablespoons sugar
3 cups buttermilk
12 ounces whipped topping

Drain the pineapple, reserving the juice. Heat the reserved pineapple juice, gelatin and sugar in a saucepan until dissolved. Beat the pineapple in a bowl until mashed. Stir in the gelatin mixture and buttermilk and mix well. Add the whipped topping. Beat at low speed until mixed well. Spoon into a serving dish. Chill until set. May substitute peach gelatin for the apricot gelatin. *Yield: 6 to 8 servings.*

Marilyn Wilkins

Congealed Cranberry Salad

2 cups ground cranberries
2 cups sugar
2 (3-ounce) packages lemon gelatin
2 cups hot water
2 cups pineapple juice
2 cups chopped celery
2 cups drained crushed pineapple
1 cup chopped nuts

Combine the cranberries and sugar in a bowl and set aside. Dissolve the gelatin in hot water in a bowl. Stir in the pineapple juice. Chill until partially set. Fold in the cranberries, celery, pineapple and nuts. Spoon into a serving dish. Chill until set. *Yield: 6 to 8 servings.*

Nell Horn

Frozen Cranberry Salad

8 ounces cream cheese, softened
1/2 cup sugar
1 tablespoon lemon juice
1/2 cup nuts (optional)
1 (16-ounce) can whole cranberry sauce
9 ounces whipped topping

Beat the cream cheese and sugar in a bowl until light and fluffy. Beat in the lemon juice. Fold in the nuts and cranberry sauce. Fold in the whipped topping. Pour into a 1-quart salad mold or a 5x9-inch loaf pan sprayed with nonstick cooking spray. Freeze, covered with plastic wrap, for 24 hours. Remove from the freezer just before serving. Unmold onto a serving plate and garnish with green grapes. *Yield: 12 to 15 servings.*

Carmen Golden

Five-Cup Salad

1 cup chopped apples
1 cup orange sections
1 cup miniature marshmallows
1 cup shredded coconut
1 cup sour cream

Combine the apples, oranges, marshmallows and coconut in a bowl. Fold in the sour cream. Spoon into a serving bowl. Chill, covered, for 2 to 3 hours. May add chopped cherries. *Yield: 4 to 6 servings.*

Irene Davis

Lime Cream Cheese Salad

1 (3-ounce) package lime gelatin
1 cup hot water
1/2 cup crushed pineapple
1 envelope whipped topping mix
3 ounces cream cheese, softened

Dissolve the gelatin in hot water in a bowl. Chill until partially set. Stir in the pineapple and return to the refrigerator. Prepare the whipped topping mix using package directions. Beat in the cream cheese. Add to the gelatin mixture and blend well. Spoon into a serving bowl. Chill until set. Garnish with candied cherries. *Yield: 4 to 6 servings.*

June Brown

Mandarin Orange Salad

2 (3-ounce) packages orange gelatin
2 cups boiling water
1 pint orange sherbet
1 (11-ounce) can mandarin oranges, drained
Creamy Citrus Filling

Dissolve the orange gelatin in the boiling water in a bowl. Stir in the sherbet. Add the oranges. Pour into a ring salad mold. Chill until firm. Unmold onto a lettuce-lined salad plate. Fill the center with Creamy Citrus Filling. *Yield: 8 to 10 servings.*

Creamy Citrus Filling

1/2 cup whipping cream
1 (15-ounce) can pineapple tidbits, drained
1 (11-ounce) can mandarin oranges, drained
1 cup flaked coconut
1 cup miniature marshmallows

Whip the cream in a mixer bowl until soft peaks form. Fold in the pineapple, oranges, coconut and marshmallows.

Florence Vance

Raspberry Salad

1 (10-ounce) package frozen raspberries, thawed
1 (3-ounce) package raspberry gelatin
1/2 cup hot water
1 cup applesauce
1 cup sour cream
3/4 cup miniature marshmallows
1 tablespoon mayonnaise

Drain the raspberries, reserving 1/2 cup of the juice. Dissolve the gelatin in the hot water in a bowl. Stir in the applesauce, raspberries and the reserved juice. Pour into five 6-ounce salad molds. Chill until firm. Combine the sour cream, marshmallows and mayonnaise in a bowl and mix well. Chill until serving time. Unmold the gelatin onto lettuce-lined serving plates. Spoon the sour cream dressing over each. *Yield: 5 servings.*

Ruth Clark

Strawberry Sour Cream Gelatin Mold

1 (3-ounce) package strawberry gelatin
1 (3-ounce) package lemon gelatin
2 cups boiling water
2 (10-ounce) packages frozen sliced strawberries
2 large bananas, mashed
1 (8-ounce) can juice-pack crushed pineapple
1 cup sour cream

Dissolve the gelatins in the boiling water in a bowl. Add the frozen strawberries, bananas and undrained pineapple and mix well. Pour half the mixture into a salad mold. Chill until set. Spread the congealed layer with sour cream. Add the remaining gelatin mixture. Chill until set. Unmold onto a serving plate. *Yield: 6 to 8 servings.*

Maxine Miles

Waldorf Salad

1 (6-ounce) package lemon gelatin
1 1/2 cups boiling water
1 cup mayonnaise
1 tablespoon lemon juice
1 cup chopped unpeeled apples
1/2 cup chopped celery
1/2 cup chopped walnuts
1 small jar chopped stuffed olives, drained

Dissolve the lemon gelatin in the boiling water in a bowl. Cool to room temperature. Beat in the mayonnaise and lemon juice. Chill until partially set. Stir in the apples, celery, walnuts and olives. Spoon into a salad mold. Chill until set. *Yield: 6 to 8 servings.*

Mrs. E. J. Harmon

Watergate Salad

1 (8-ounce) can juice-pack crushed pineapple
1 (3-ounce) package instant pistachio pudding mix
1 cup miniature marshmallows
8 ounces whipped topping

Drain the pineapple, reserving the juice. Combine the reserved juice with the pudding mix in a bowl and mix well. Stir in the pineapple and marshmallows. Fold in the whipped topping. Spoon into a serving bowl. Chill, covered, until serving time. *Yield: 8 to 10 servings.*

Joanne Zwolinski

Hot Chicken Salad

1 1/2 cups chopped cooked chicken
1 1/2 cups chopped celery
1 tablespoon minced onion
1/2 cup chopped pecans
3/4 cup mayonnaise-type salad dressing
Crushed potato chips

Combine the chicken, celery, onion, pecans and salad dressing in a bowl and mix well. Layer the chicken mixture and potato chips 1/2 at a time in a greased baking dish. Bake at 450 degrees for 15 minutes. *Yield: 6 to 8 servings.*

Selma Dufina

Shrimp Salad

2 tablespoons unflavored gelatin
1/2 cup cold water
1 (10-ounce) can tomato soup
8 to 9 ounces cream cheese, softened
1 cup mayonnaise
1 1/2 cups chopped celery
1 1/2 cups chopped onion
1 1/2 cups finely chopped green bell peppers
1/2 teaspoon salt
1 tablespoon lemon juice
Chopped shrimp

Soften the gelatin in the cold water. Bring the soup to a boil in a saucepan. Add the cream cheese, stirring until melted. Add the gelatin mixture, stirring until dissolved. Let stand until cool. Stir in the mayonnaise, celery, onion, green peppers, salt, lemon juice and shrimp. Spoon into individual salad molds. Chill until set. Unmold onto lettuce-lined salad plates. *Yield: 4 to 6 servings.*

Mary Miller

Marinated Bean Salad

1 cup drained kidney beans
1 cup drained green beans
1 cup drained wax beans
Chopped green bell pepper
Chopped onions
Chopped pimento (optional)
¾ cup sugar
1 teaspoon salt
½ teaspoon pepper
⅓ cup salad oil
⅔ cup vinegar

Rinse the kidney beans under cold water and drain well. Combine with the green beans and wax beans in a bowl. Add the green pepper, onions and pimento and mix well. Mix the sugar, salt, pepper, salad oil and vinegar in a bowl. Add to the bean mixture and mix well. Marinate, covered, in the refrigerator for several hours to overnight. Drain before serving. *Yield: 6 to 8 servings.*

Helga R. Doud

String Bean Salad

1½ pounds string beans
Sliced or minced fresh onion
½ cup plus 2 tablespoons sugar
½ cup vinegar
½ cup water

Rinse and trim the beans. Cut into pieces and place in a saucepan with onion and water to cover. Cook until tender-crisp and drain. Place in a bowl. Dissolve the sugar in vinegar and ½ cup water in a bowl. Pour over the hot beans. Marinate, covered, in the refrigerator overnight. *Yield: 6 to 8 servings.*

Carl Nold

Broccoli Bacon Salad

1 large bunch broccoli, cut into florets	1 small red onion, coarsely chopped	3 tablespoons vinegar
1 cup raisins	10 to 12 slices bacon, crisp-fried, crumbled	1/3 cup mayonnaise
		1/3 cup sugar

Combine the broccoli, raisins, red onion and bacon in a large bowl. Add a mixture of the vinegar, mayonnaise and sugar and toss to coat. *Yield: 6 to 8 servings.*

Rosemary Lounsbury

Spinach Salad

1 (16-ounce) package spinach, torn	8 ounces bacon, crisp-fried, crumbled	1 or 2 hard-cooked eggs, sliced, crumbled
2 cups chopped lettuce	1/2 cup sliced green onion tops	Spinach Salad Dressing

Toss the spinach and lettuce in a large bowl. Sprinkle with the bacon, green onion tops and eggs. Add the Spinach Salad Dressing and toss carefully. *Yield: 8 to 10 servings.*

Spinach Salad Dressing

1 egg	1/2 cup red wine vinegar	2 tablespoons melted bacon drippings
1/2 cup sugar	3/4 teaspoon salt	

Process the egg in a food processor. Add the sugar, vinegar, salt and bacon drippings and process until blended.

Lornie Porter

Italian Tomato Salad

3 large tomatoes, chopped
2 green onions with tops, sliced
1 green bell pepper, thinly sliced
¼ cup salad oil
⅛ teaspoon vinegar
¼ teaspoon oregano
Salt and pepper to taste

Combine the tomatoes, green onions and green pepper in a bowl. Add a mixture of the salad oil, vinegar, oregano, salt and pepper and toss well. Chill, covered, in the refrigerator. Yield: 4 to 6 servings.

Anne St. Onge

Tomato Aspic Salad

1 (3-ounce) package lemon gelatin
1 cup boiling water
1 (8-ounce) can tomato sauce
2 tablespoons vinegar
⅛ teaspoon Worcestershire sauce
⅛ teaspoon salt
⅛ teaspoon pepper
Sliced stuffed olives
Sliced hard-cooked eggs
2½ tablespoons shredded cabbage
2½ tablespoons chopped celery
2½ tablespoons chopped green bell pepper
2½ tablespoons shredded carrot
2½ tablespoons chopped cucumber
2½ tablespoons chopped onion

Dissolve the gelatin in the boiling water in a bowl. Stir in the tomato sauce, vinegar, Worcestershire sauce, salt and pepper. Arrange the stuffed olives and a slice of hard-cooked egg in 6 to 8 individual salad molds. Pour a small amount of the gelatin mixture into each mold. Chill until set. Stir the vegetables into the remaining gelatin. Pour into the prepared salad molds. Chill until set. May add chopped cooked chicken, shrimp or cottage cheese to the gelatin mixture. May also dissolve a bouillon cube with the gelatin in the boiling water. Yield: 6 to 8 servings.

Helen Pfeiffelman

Wonderful Vegetable Salad

1 (16-ounce) can French-style green beans, drained
1 (16-ounce) can fancy Chinese vegetables, drained
1 (16-ounce) can small green peas, drained
1 (8-ounce) can sliced water chestnuts, drained
1 1/2 cups thinly sliced celery
3 medium onions, thinly sliced
1 cup sugar
3/4 cup cider vinegar
Salt and pepper to taste

Combine the vegetables in a large bowl. Add a mixture of the sugar, vinegar, salt and pepper and mix well. Chill, covered, in the refrigerator for several hours. *Yield: 10 to 12 servings.*

Arleen Kirkland

Celery Seed Salad Dressing

2/3 cup sugar
1 teaspoon dry mustard
1 teaspoon salt
1/3 cup vinegar
1 cup vegetable oil, chilled
1/4 teaspoon grated onion
1 teaspoon celery seeds

Combine the sugar, mustard, salt and vinegar in a bowl and mix well. Chill in the refrigerator. Add the chilled oil gradually to the chilled vinegar mixture, beating constantly. Add the onion and celery seeds and beat well. Store in the refrigerator. *Yield: 1 to 1 1/2 cups.*

Josephine Bay

Creamy Salad Dressing

3 egg yolks
1 teaspoon flour
1 teaspoon dry mustard
5 teaspoons sugar
1/4 teaspoon salt
1/4 cup vinegar
2 tablespoons butter
Evaporated milk

Mix the egg yolks, flour, mustard, sugar and salt with enough water in a double boiler to make a paste. Add the vinegar. Cook over boiling water until thickened, stirring constantly. Stir in the butter. Let stand until cool. Beat in enough evaporated milk until of the desired consistency. *Yield: 3/4 to 1 cup.*

Jeanette Doud

Green Goddess Salad Dressing

1 cup mayonnaise	3 tablespoons chives, chopped	3 tablespoons tarragon vinegar
1/2 cup sour cream		1 tablespoon lemon juice
1/2 cup chopped parsley	3 tablespoons anchovy paste	Salt and pepper to taste
1 clove of garlic, chopped		

Combine the mayonnaise, sour cream, parsley, garlic, chives, anchovy paste, vinegar, lemon juice, salt and pepper in a bowl and mix well. Chill overnight. *Yield: 1 pint.*

Betty Brown

Honey Dressing for Fruit Salad

2/3 cup sugar	5 tablespoons vinegar	1/3 cup strained honey
1 teaspoon paprika	1 tablespoon catsup	1 teaspoon grated onion
1 teaspoon celery salt	1 teaspoon mustard	2/3 cup salad oil
	1/2 teaspoon salt	

Combine the sugar, paprika, celery salt, vinegar, catsup, mustard, salt, honey, onion and salad oil in a bowl. Beat for 20 minutes or until thick. Chill in the refrigerator. *Yield: 1 1/2 to 2 cups.*

Maxine Miles

Roquefort Dressing

1 cup sour cream	1 package of Roquefort cheese, crumbled	Vinegar
1 cup mayonnaise		Crushed garlic

Combine the sour cream and mayonnaise in a bowl. Stir in the cheese. Add a small amount of vinegar and garlic and mix well. May use Danish Bleu cheese instead of the Roquefort cheese. *Yield: 2 to 2 1/2 cups.*

Mrs. George Clark

Satisfying Main Events

Entrées & Side Dishes

Italian Beef Steaks

4 sirloin steaks,
1/4 inch thick
Vegetable oil
Seasoned bread crumbs

1 medium onion, cut into
1-inch pieces

4 slices mozzarella cheese,
cut into 1-inch pieces
4 slices tomato
4 slices margarine

Dip the steaks in the oil and then in the bread crumbs, coating each side well. Place the onion pieces, cheese pieces, 1 tomato slice and 1 slice of margarine on each steak. Fold each steak over to enclose the filling and secure with wooden picks. Place on a broiler pan. Broil on each side until the steaks are done to taste. Serve immediately. *Yield: 4 servings.*

Carolyn Metting

Pot Roast

1 (3- to 4-pound)
pot roast

2 tablespoons A.1.
steak sauce
1 envelope onion
soup mix

1 (10-ounce) can cream of
mushroom soup

Place the pot roast on a large piece of foil. Brush the pot roast with the steak sauce. Sprinkle with the onion soup mix. Spread the mushroom soup over the pot roast. Wrap in the foil. Place in a baking pan. Bake at 350 degrees for 2 1/2 hours or until done to taste. *Yield: 4 to 6 servings.*

Mary Rogers

Lemon Pepper Steak

1 eye-of-round roast

Lemon pepper to taste

Rub the roast with the lemon pepper. Place in a baking dish. Bake, covered, at 450 degrees for 15 minutes. Reduce the oven temperature to 275 degrees. Bake for 4 hours longer. *Yield: variable.*

Virginia Bennetts

Sukiyaki

1 1/2 pounds steak, thinly sliced
2 tablespoons vegetable oil
3/4 cup soy sauce
1/4 cup mushroom stock or water
1/4 cup sugar
2 medium onions, sliced
1 green bell pepper, julienned
1 cup 1 1/2-inch julienned celery
1 (8-ounce) can bamboo shoots, thinly sliced
1 (6-ounce) can sliced mushrooms
1 bunch green onions with tops, cut into 1-inch pieces
1/2 cup sake (optional)

Brown the steak in the hot oil in a large skillet. Mix the soy sauce, mushroom stock and sugar in a bowl. Add half the mixture to the steak. Move the steak to 1 side of the skillet and add the onions, green pepper and celery. Cook for a few minutes. Add the remaining soy sauce mixture, bamboo shoots and mushrooms. Cook for 3 to 5 minutes. Add the green onions. Cook for 1 minute. Stir in the sake. Cook for 1 minute, stirring constantly. Serve immediately with or on top of hot cooked rice. May cook in an electric skillet right at the dinner table. *Yield: 8 servings.*

Mary Plunkett

Lazy-Day Beef Casserole

1 1/2 pounds stew beef, cut into 2-inch pieces
1/2 cup red wine
1 (10-ounce) can consommé
1/8 teaspoon pepper
1 medium onion, sliced
1/4 cup fine dry bread crumbs
1/4 cup flour

Combine the stew beef, wine, consommé, pepper and onion in a bowl. Stir in the bread crumbs and flour. Spoon into a baking dish. Bake, covered, at 300 degrees for 3 hours or until the stew beef is tender. *Yield: 4 servings.*

Marsha Kleber

My Mother's Chili

5 small onions, finely chopped
1 cup butter
2 pounds round steak, ground
1 teaspoon salt
1/4 teaspoon pepper
1 1/2 teaspoons chili powder, or to taste
1 (15-ounce) can tomatoes
1 (10-ounce) can tomato soup
1 (16-ounce) can kidney beans or chili beans

Brown the onions in the butter in a skillet. Add the ground round. Cook until the ground round is brown and crumbly, stirring constantly. Add the salt, pepper, chili powder, tomatoes, tomato soup and beans and mix well. Bring to a boil. Boil for 10 minutes and reduce heat. Simmer for 1 hour. *Yield: 6 to 8 servings.*

Connie Duey

Bob-Lo Barbecue Bean Bake

1 pound ground beef
1 pound bacon, chopped
1 large onion, chopped
1/2 cup catsup
1/2 cup barbecue sauce
1 teaspoon salt
1/4 cup prepared mustard
1/4 cup molasses
1 tablespoon chili powder
3/4 teaspoon pepper
2 (16-ounce) cans red kidney beans
2 (16-ounce) cans pork and beans
2 (16-ounce) cans butter beans

Brown the ground beef with the bacon and onion in a large saucepan, stirring until the ground beef is crumbly; drain. Stir in the catsup, barbecue sauce, salt, mustard, molasses, chili powder and pepper. Add the beans and mix well. Pour into a large baking dish. Bake at 350 degrees for 1 hour. May also cook in a large slow cooker. *Yield: 15 to 20 servings.*

Don Francis

Ground Beef Goulash

8 ounces egg noodles
1 pound lean ground beef
1/2 cup chopped onion
1/2 cup sliced celery
1 clove of garlic, chopped
1 (15-ounce) can stewed tomatoes
1 (8-ounce) can tomato paste
1 1/2 cups water
1 teaspoon paprika
1 teaspoon Worcestershire sauce
1/2 teaspoon each pepper, salt and sugar

Cook the noodles in a saucepan using the package directions and set aside. Brown the ground beef in a large skillet over medium heat, stirring until crumbly; drain. Add the onion, celery and garlic. Cook until tender, stirring constantly. Stir in the tomatoes, tomato paste, water, paprika, Worcestershire sauce, pepper, salt and sugar. Bring to a boil and reduce heat. Simmer, covered, for 30 minutes. Drain the noodles. Stir the noodles into the ground beef mixture. Cook until heated through. Serve immediately. *Yield: 4 to 6 servings.*

Stephanie and Andrew McGreevy

Cheesy Ground Beef Casserole

2 1/2 cups noodles
3 tablespoons melted butter or margarine
1 cup cottage cheese
6 ounces cream cheese
1/3 cup sour cream
2 tablespoons chopped green bell pepper
1/3 cup minced onion
1 tablespoon drained chopped pimento
1 tablespoon chopped chives
1/4 teaspoon salt
1/2 teaspoon MSG
12 ounces ground beef
1 to 2 tablespoons butter or margarine
2 (8-ounce) cans tomato sauce, or 2 cups
1/2 teaspoon salt
1/2 teaspoon Worcestershire sauce
3 drops of Tabasco sauce

Cook the noodles in a saucepan using the package directions and drain. Add 3 tablespoons melted butter and toss to coat. Set aside the noodles in a warm place. Beat the cottage cheese, cream cheese and sour cream in a bowl until smooth. Add the green pepper, onion, pimento, chives, 1/4 teaspoon salt and MSG and mix well. Brown the ground beef in 1 to 2 tablespoons butter in a heavy skillet over medium heat, stirring until crumbly; drain. Stir in the tomato sauce, 1/2 teaspoon salt, Worcestershire sauce and Tabasco sauce. Pour a small amount into a greased 2-quart baking dish. Layer half the noodles, cheese mixture, remaining noodles and remaining ground beef mixture in the prepared dish. Bake at 350 degrees for 50 to 60 minutes or until bubbly. *Yield: 6 servings.*

Chris Bazinaw

Spaghetti

1 to 1 1/2 pounds ground chuck
2 tablespoons vegetable oil
1 medium onion, chopped
1 large green bell pepper, chopped
4 medium carrots, shredded
3 ribs celery, chopped
1/3 cup finely chopped fresh parsley
2 (10-ounce) cans tomato soup
2 (6-ounce) cans tomato paste
2 or 3 tomato paste cans water
1 teaspoon finely chopped fresh oregano
1/8 teaspoon allspice
Salt and pepper to taste
8 ounces thin spaghetti, cooked, drained
Grated Romano cheese to taste
1/8 teaspoon garlic powder

Shape the ground beef into small balls. Brown the meatballs in the vegetable oil in a skillet. Remove from the skillet to a bowl. Set aside in the refrigerator. Combine the onion, green pepper, carrots, celery, parsley, tomato soup, tomato paste, water, oregano, allspice, salt and pepper in a large saucepan and mix well. Simmer gently for 2 hours, stirring frequently. Add the meatballs. Simmer gently for 30 minutes or until cooked through. Spoon over the hot spaghetti. Sprinkle with the cheese and garlic powder. *Yield: 4 to 6 servings.*

Madeline Cowles

Ground Beef Stroganoff

1/2 cup minced onion
1/4 cup butter or margarine
1 pound ground beef
1 clove of garlic, minced
2 tablespoons flour
2 teaspoons salt
1/4 teaspoon MSG
1/4 teaspoon pepper
1/2 teaspoon paprika
1 (8-ounce) can mushroom stems and pieces
1 (10-ounce) can cream of chicken soup or cream of mushroom soup
1 cup sour cream
Snipped fresh parsley, chives or dillweed

Sauté the onion in the butter in a skillet until golden brown. Stir in the ground beef, garlic, flour, salt, MSG, pepper, paprika and mushrooms. Sauté for 5 minutes or until the ground beef is brown and crumbly. Add the soup. Simmer for 10 minutes. Stir in the sour cream. Sprinkle with the parsley. Serve over hot mashed potatoes, rice, noodles or toast. *Yield: 4 to 6 servings.*

Mrs. Kirby Samuels

Open-Faced Hamburgers

1 pound ground beef
4 ounces Velveeta cheese, chopped
2 to 3 tablespoons grated onion
1 egg
Salt and pepper to taste
4 hamburger buns, split

Combine the ground beef, cheese, onion, egg, salt and pepper in a bowl and mix well. Spread the ground beef mixture on the hamburger bun halves. Place on a broiler pan. Broil until brown and the ground beef is cooked through. Serve with favorite condiments such as catsup, pickles and mustard. *Yield: 4 servings.*

Elizabeth Sieffert

Meatballs

2 pounds ground beef
1 cup crushed cornflakes
1/3 cup chopped parsley
2 eggs
2 tablespoons soy sauce
1/2 teaspoon garlic salt
1/2 cup catsup
2 tablespoons onion flakes
Chili and Cranberry Sauce

Combine the ground beef, cornflakes, parsley, eggs, soy sauce, garlic salt, catsup and onion flakes in a bowl and mix well. Shape into 1-inch meatballs. Place in a 9x13-inch baking pan. Pour the Chili and Cranberry Sauce over the meatballs. Bake at 350 degrees for 1 hour or until the meatballs are cooked through. Bake at 325 degrees if using a glass baking dish. *Yield: 6 to 8 servings.*

Chili and Cranberry Sauce

1 (8-ounce) can jellied cranberry sauce
1 tablespoon lemon juice
1 (12-ounce) bottle chili sauce
2 tablespoons brown sugar

Combine the cranberry sauce, lemon juice, chili sauce and brown sugar in a saucepan. Cook over low heat until melted, stirring constantly.

Barb Chaffee

Norwegian Meatballs

2 pounds ground round steak
2 small onions, finely chopped
Butter
2 teaspoons cornstarch
4 Holland rusks, crushed, or 8 zwieback, crushed
2 teaspoons salt
2 teaspoons brown sugar
1/2 teaspoon pepper
1/2 cup milk
1/2 cup cream
1 egg, beaten
1/2 cup butter
3 tablespoons flour
5 bouillon cubes
3 cups hot water

Have the butcher grind the ground round steak a second time until very finely ground. Brown the onions in a small amount of butter in a skillet. Combine the ground round, onions, cornstarch, Holland rusks, salt, brown sugar, pepper, milk, cream and egg in a large bowl and mix well. Shape into 1 1/2-inch balls.

Brown the meatballs in 1/2 cup butter in a skillet. Remove the meatballs to a bowl with a slotted spoon. Stir the flour into the pan drippings. Cook until brown, stirring constantly. Add the bouillon cubes and hot water. Cook until the bouillon cubes are dissolved, stirring constantly. Return the meatballs to the skillet. Simmer for 15 minutes or until the meatballs are cooked through. Serve with a large platter of boiled potatoes, peas, carrots and cauliflower. Garnish with parsley. *Yield: 8 servings.*

Josephine Bay

Swedish Meatballs

5 ounces ground pork
11 ounces ground beef
1 cup bread crumbs
2 1/2 cups milk
1 tablespoon grated onion
1 1/2 teaspoons salt
1 teaspoon pepper
1 egg
1/8 teaspoon ginger
Margarine for browning
Chopped parsley

Combine the ground pork, ground beef, bread crumbs, milk, onion, salt, pepper, egg and ginger in a large bowl and mix well. Shape into 1 1/2-inch balls. Cook in the margarine in a skillet until brown and cooked through. Remove the meatballs to a serving platter. Make a gravy using the pan drippings. Pour over the meatballs and sprinkle with chopped fresh parsley. Serve with boiled potatoes, noodles and/or carrots. *Yield: 6 servings.*

Birgit Madsen

Meat Pasties

3 cups sifted flour
¾ cup mixed shortening and lard

¼ cup scraped suet
1¼ pounds sirloin steak, chopped
4 medium potatoes, sliced

2 medium onions, sliced
¼ cup sliced rutabaga
Salt and pepper to taste

Sift the flour into a bowl. Cut in the shortening and lard mixture and suet until course crumbs are formed. Add just enough water to make a soft dough. Divide the dough into 4 portions. Roll each portion into a large circle on a lightly floured surface. Combine the steak, potatoes, onions and rutabaga in a bowl and mix well. Divide the mixture into 4 portions. Place each portion on half of each circle. Sprinkle with salt and pepper. Fold the remaining half of the pastry over the filling and press the edge to seal. Place on a baking sheet. Bake at 375 degrees for 30 to 35 minutes. Reduce the oven temperature to 350 degrees. Bake for 15 minutes longer. *Yield: 4 servings.*

Ada Chambers

Meat Pie

1 pound very lean round steak, ground 3 times
1½ cups cold water

2 medium onions, finely chopped
Sifted flour

Salt to taste
1 recipe (2-crust) pie pastry

Combine the ground steak, cold water and onions in a saucepan. Bring to a boil and reduce heat. Simmer for 2 to 3 hours, stirring occasionally. Add just enough flour to thicken, stirring constantly. Cook until thickened, stirring constantly. Season with salt. Pour into a pastry-lined pie plate. Top with the remaining pastry, sealing and fluting the edge and cutting vents. Bake at 450 degrees for 10 minutes. Reduce the oven temperature to 350 degrees. Bake for 30 minutes longer or until golden brown. *Yield: 6 to 8 servings.*

Sally Dufina

Scotch Meat Pie

1 1/2 pounds ground beef
2 cups cold water
2 onions, sliced
2 tablespoons flour
2 tablespoons water
1 teaspoon Worcestershire sauce
1/2 teaspoon ginger
1/2 teaspoon poultry seasoning
Salt and pepper to taste
Scotch Meat Pie Pastry

Place the ground beef in a large saucepan. Add 2 cups water, stirring to separate the ground beef. Add the onions. Simmer for 1 hour. Mix the flour, 2 tablespoons water, Worcestershire sauce, ginger, poultry seasoning, salt and pepper in a bowl. Stir into the ground beef mixture. Cook for 15 minutes. Line a pie plate with half the Scotch Meat Pie Pastry. Add the ground beef filling. Top with the remaining Scotch Meat Pie Pastry, sealing and fluting the edge and cutting vents. Brush the top with cold water. Bake at 400 degrees for 10 minutes. Reduce the oven temperature to 350 degrees. Bake for 35 minutes longer. Yield: 6 to 8 servings.

Scotch Meat Pie Pastry

2 cups flour
1 teaspoon salt
2/3 cup shortening
5 tablespoons water

Sift the flour and salt into a bowl. Cut in the shortening until crumbly. Add the water gradually, stirring until a soft dough forms. Divide the dough into 2 portions. Roll each portion into a thin circle on a lightly floured surface.

Agnes Shine

French-Canadian Meat Pie

1 (3-pound) chicken or fowl, cut up	2 tablespoons minced parsley	1 bay leaf
Vegetable oil	1 onion, chopped	1/8 teaspoon salt
1/2 cup chopped celery	1 whole clove	2 pounds minced pork
1 carrot, chopped	Thyme and marjoram to taste	French-Canadian Meat Pie Pastry

Rinse the chicken and pat dry. Brown the chicken in a small amount of vegetable oil in a skillet. Add the celery, carrot, parsley, onion, clove, thyme, marjoram, bay leaf and salt. Add just enough water to cover. Cook until the chicken is tender. Drain the chicken, reserving the broth. Strain the broth, returning the seasonings to the chicken. Brown the pork in a skillet, stirring until crumbly. Add the reserved chicken broth. Cook for about 2 hours.

Remove and discard the skin and bones from the chicken. Add the chicken pieces and seasonings to the pork and mix well. Let stand until cool. Discard the bay leaf and clove. Line a deep-dish pie plate with half the French-Canadian Meat Pie Pastry. Add the chicken mixture. Top with the remaining French-Canadian Meat Pie Pastry, sealing and fluting the edge and cutting vents. Bake at 450 degrees until the top is golden brown. Reduce the oven temperature to 350 degrees. Bake for 1 hour longer. *Yield: 6 to 8 servings.*

French-Canadian Meat Pie Pastry

1 1/2 cups flour	1 teaspoon salt	6 teaspoons shortening

Sift the flour and salt in a bowl. Cut in the shortening until crumbly. Add just enough cold water to form a soft dough. Chill, covered, for 15 minutes. Divide the pastry into 2 equal portions. Roll each portion into a large circle on a lightly floured surface.

Simone Vuignier

Quick Lamb Curry

¼ cup vegetable oil
1 onion, thinly sliced
5 cloves of garlic, chopped
1 apple, chopped
1 green bell pepper, chopped

½ cup raisins
¼ cup chopped dried apricots
2 tablespoons salted peanuts (optional)
1½ to 2 cups chopped lamb

1 cup apple juice
Juice of 1 lemon
1 tablespoon cinnamon
2 tablespoons curry powder
¼ cup skim milk

Heat the vegetable oil in a large skillet. Add the onion and garlic. Sauté until the onion is translucent. Stir in the apple, green pepper, raisins, apricots and peanuts. Add the lamb. Cook until the lamb is light brown. Add the apple juice, lemon juice, cinnamon and curry powder. Reduce the heat. Stir in the milk. Simmer, covered, for 15 to 20 minutes. Serve over basmati rice and garnish with lime wedges. *Yield: 4 to 6 servings.*

Candi Dunnigan

Smothered Potatoes

2 or 3 pork steaks
Vegetable oil

2 tablespoons flour
1 medium onion, sliced

5 medium baking potatoes, peeled, sliced

Brown the pork steaks in a small amount of vegetable oil in a heavy skillet. Remove the steaks to a platter. Stir the flour into the pan drippings. Add just enough water to make a light gravy. Layer the onion and potatoes in a baking dish. Arrange the steaks over the layers. Pour the gravy over the top. Bake, covered, at 350 degrees for 1½ hours or until the steaks are cooked through. Serve with chilled applesauce. *Yield: 2 to 3 servings.*

Kathleen Hoppenrath

Barbecued Spareribs

5 pounds lean baby spareribs	1/2 cup chopped celery	1 teaspoon cumin seeds
Salt and pepper to taste	2 tablespoons bacon drippings	2 tablespoons Worcestershire sauce
Paprika to taste	1/2 cup cooked tomatoes	2 tablespoons sugar
2 cups vinegar	1/2 cup tomato paste	2 tablespoons chili powder
1 cup sherry	2 cups vinegar	
2 cloves of garlic, minced	1 tablespoon dry mustard	1/8 teaspoon Tabasco sauce
2 large onions, minced	1 teaspoon dried thyme	

Season the spareribs with salt, pepper and paprika and place in a shallow glass dish. Pour a mixture of 2 cups vinegar, wine and garlic over the spareribs. Marinate, covered, in the refrigerator for several hours to overnight, turning the spareribs once or twice.

Sauté the onions and celery in the bacon drippings in a skillet until the onions are translucent. Add the tomatoes, tomato paste, 2 cups vinegar, dry mustard, thyme, cumin seeds, Worcestershire sauce, sugar, chili powder and Tabasco sauce and mix well. Bring to a boil. Boil for 2 minutes. Drain the spareribs, discarding the marinade. Brush with some of the sauce. Place the spareribs on a grill rack. Grill over hot coals until the spareribs are brown and cooked through, basting with the sauce every 10 minutes. *Yield: 4 to 6 servings.*

Arlene Chambers

Ham Loaf

2 eggs, lightly beaten
1/2 cup milk
1 cup bran flakes
3/4 teaspoon dry mustard

1 teaspoon Worcestershire sauce
4 cups finely ground cooked ham

3 tablespoons brown sugar
1 tablespoon melted butter

Mix the eggs, milk, cereal, dry mustard and Worcestershire sauce in a bowl. Add the ham and mix well. Mix the brown sugar and butter in a bowl. Spread over the bottom of a 5x9-inch loaf pan. Pack the ham mixture firmly into the prepared pan. Bake at 350 degrees for 1 hour. May pack the ham mixture into 6 muffin or custard cups, using the butter and brown sugar as a glaze, and bake for 40 minutes. *Yield: 6 servings.*

Mable Breuckman

Scalloped Ham and Egg Casserole

2 cups cubed cooked ham
1 (10-ounce) can cream of mushroom soup

1 cup evaporated milk
1/4 cup water
4 hard-cooked eggs, chopped

Crushed potato chips
1 tablespoon melted shortening

Combine the ham, mushroom soup, evaporated milk, water and eggs in a bowl and mix well. Spoon into a greased 1 1/2-quart casserole. Sprinkle a mixture of potato chips and shortening over the top. Bake at 375 degrees for 20 minutes. *Yield: 4 to 6 servings.*

Joanne Zwolinski

Breakfast Surprise

1 1/2 pounds bulk pork sausage
9 eggs, lightly beaten
3 cups milk
1 1/2 teaspoons dry mustard (optional)
1 teaspoon salt
3 slices white bread, cubed
1 1/2 cups shredded Cheddar cheese

Brown the sausage in a skillet, stirring until crumbly; drain. Combine the eggs, milk, dry mustard and salt in a large bowl. Stir in the bread, sausage and cheese. Pour into a lightly greased 9x13-inch baking dish. Chill, covered, overnight. Bake, uncovered, at 350 degrees for 1 hour. Cut into squares and serve with homemade biscuits. *Yield: 12 servings.*

Karen Culbert

Surprise Soufflé

1 1/2 pounds bulk sausage
9 eggs
3 cups milk
1 1/2 teaspoons salt
1/8 teaspoon pepper
1 1/2 teaspoons dry mustard
12 slices bread, cubed
1 1/2 cups grated sharp Cheddar cheese
1 teaspoon paprika

Brown the sausage in a skillet, stirring until crumbly; drain. Let stand until cool. Beat the eggs, milk, salt, pepper and dry mustard in a large bowl. Stir in the bread cubes. Add the sausage and cheese and mix well. Pour into a 9x13-inch glass baking dish. Chill, covered, overnight. Remove from the refrigerator 1 hour before baking. Sprinkle with the paprika. Bake at 350 degrees for 45 minutes or until set. Let stand for 15 minutes before serving. May be frozen. *Yield: 6 to 10 servings.*

Patti Ann Moskwa

Coddle

6 slices bacon, cut into 1-inch pieces
1 tablespoon vegetable oil
2 large onions, chopped
2 cloves of garlic, crushed
8 large pork sausages
4 large potatoes, sliced
¼ teaspoon sage
⅛ teaspoon salt
Pepper to taste
1¼ cups chicken stock
2 tablespoons chopped fresh parsley (optional)

Fry the bacon in the vegetable oil in a skillet for 2 minutes. Add the onions. Cook for 5 minutes. Add the garlic. Cook for several minutes and set aside. Brown the sausages in a nonstick skillet. Place the potatoes in a buttered glass baking dish or cast-iron skillet. Layer the bacon mixture and sausages over the potatoes. Sprinkle with the sage, salt and pepper. Pour the chicken stock over the layers. Bake at 350 degrees for 30 to 40 minutes or until the sausages are cooked through and the potatoes are tender. Sprinkle with parsley. Serve with a loaf of homemade bread. May substitute bratwurst, venison, Italian, kielbasa, knackwurst or Polish sausages for the pork sausages. *Yield: 4 servings.*

Daniel Wade Seeley

Italian Vegetable Casserole

1 medium eggplant, peeled, cubed
1 red bell pepper, thinly sliced lengthwise
1 yellow bell pepper, thinly sliced lengthwise
1 cup thinly sliced mushrooms
1 red onion, thinly sliced lengthwise
2 tablespoons olive oil
1 pound spicy hot Italian sausage
3 cups meatless spaghetti sauce
½ cup plus 2 tablespoons seasoned Italian bread crumbs
½ cup shredded mozzarella cheese

Sauté the eggplant, red pepper, yellow pepper, mushrooms and onion in the olive oil in a large skillet for 5 minutes. Remove from the skillet and set aside. Crumble the sausage in the skillet and cook until brown. Add the sautéed vegetables, spaghetti sauce and ½ cup of the bread crumbs and mix well. Spray a large casserole with nonstick cooking spray. Sprinkle with the remaining 2 tablespoons bread crumbs. Add the sausage mixture. Sprinkle with the mozzarella cheese. Bake at 350 degrees for 45 minutes. *Yield: 4 to 6 servings.*

Betty BeDour

Lasagna

1 pound Polish or Italian sausage, chopped or crumbled
Vegetable oil
1 clove of garlic, minced
1 tablespoon basil
1/2 teaspoon salt
1 (16-ounce) can tomatoes
2 (6-ounce) cans tomato paste
3 cups cottage cheese
1/2 cup grated Parmesan cheese
2 teaspoons parsley flakes
2 eggs, beaten
1 teaspoon salt
1/2 teaspoon pepper
10 ounces lasagna noodles
1 pound mozzarella cheese, sliced

Brown the sausage in a small amount of vegetable in a skillet oil over low heat; drain. Add the garlic, basil, salt, tomatoes and tomato paste and mix well. Simmer for 30 minutes. Combine the cottage cheese, Parmesan cheese, parsley flakes, eggs, salt and pepper in a bowl and mix well. Cook the noodles using the package directions; drain. Line a baking pan with half the noodles. Layer the cottage cheese mixture, mozzarella cheese, sausage mixture and the remaining noodles 1/2 at a time in the prepared pan. Bake at 375 degrees for 30 minutes. Let stand for 10 minutes before serving. Serve with the Dilly Bread on page 102. *Yield: 8 to 10 servings.*

Joanne Zwolinski

Bubble-Up Pizza

2 (10-count) cans buttermilk biscuits
1 1/2 cups pizza or spaghetti sauce
1 pound sausage, cooked, drained
1 (2-ounce) jar sliced green or black olives, drained
1 (8-ounce) package sliced fresh mushrooms
12 ounces shredded Cheddar cheese
1 (8-ounce) package sliced pepperoni

Tear the biscuit dough into quarters into a large bowl. Add 1 cup of the sauce, sausage, olives, mushrooms and half the cheese and mix well. Spread into a greased glass baking dish. Layer the pepperoni and remaining 1/2 cup sauce over the top. Sprinkle with the remaining cheese. Bake at 375 degrees for 25 minutes or until the sides are golden brown. *Yield: 6 to 8 servings.*

Ann Linn

Spaghetti Sauce with Italian Sausage

1 tablespoon vegetable oil
1 medium onion, finely chopped
1 pound mild Italian sausage, cut into 1-inch pieces
1 (15-ounce) can tomato sauce
1 tomato sauce can water
1 (5-ounce) can tomato paste

Heat the vegetable oil in a stockpot over medium heat. Add the onion and sausage. Sauté until the onion is transparent and the sausage is light brown; drain. Add the tomato sauce, water and tomato paste and mix well. Simmer, covered, for 1 to 1½ hours or until the sauce is thickened, stirring occasionally. Serve over hot cooked spaghetti or other pasta. Yield: 3 to 4 servings.

Anne St. Onge

Venison Steak with Stout and Potatoes

2 pounds venison or sirloin steak
Salt and pepper to taste
1 tablespoon vegetable oil
2 tablespoons butter
8 ounces baby onions or chopped onion
6 ounces stout beer
1¼ cups beef stock
1 tablespoon flour
½ teaspoon mild prepared mustard
1 bay leaf
1½ pounds potatoes, thickly sliced
10 to 16 ounces fresh mushrooms, sliced

Trim the steak and season with salt and pepper. Brown the steak in the vegetable oil and butter in a skillet, being careful not to burn the butter and vegetable oil. Remove the steak to a platter. Add the onions to the skillet. Sauté until brown. Return the steak to the skillet. Stir in the beer, beef stock, flour, mustard and bay leaf. Add the potatoes. Simmer, covered, for 30 to 60 minutes. Add the mushrooms. Cook for 30 minutes longer. Discard the bay leaf. Garnish with sprigs of thyme. Yield: 6 to 8 servings.

Daniel Wade Seeley

Venison Pie

1 1/2 pounds ground venison
1/2 cup barbecue sauce
2/3 cup dry bread crumbs
2 eggs
1/2 cup chopped onion
3 cloves of garlic, chopped
2 teaspoons sage
1 teaspoon salt
Pepper to taste
1 unbaked (10-inch) pie shell
Bacon slices

Combine the ground venison, barbecue sauce, bread crumbs, eggs, onion, garlic, sage, salt and pepper in a bowl and mix well. Spoon into the pie shell. Arrange bacon slices over the top of the pie. Bake at 350 degrees for 1 hour or until cooked through. May substitute ground beef for part of the ground venison. *Yield: 6 to 8 servings.*

Trish Martin

Chalupas

1 (3-pound) chicken, cooked
12 ounces Monterey Jack cheese, grated
12 ounces Cheddar cheese, grated
6 green onions with tops, chopped
1 (16-ounce) can sliced black olives
2 cups sour cream
1 (2-ounce) can green chiles, drained, chopped
1 (10-ounce) can cream of chicken soup
12 flour tortillas
Paprika to taste

Chop the chicken into bite-size pieces, discarding the skin and bones. Mix the Monterey Jack cheese and Cheddar cheese in a bowl. Reserve 1 cup of the cheese mixture and a few chopped green onions for the topping. Combine the remaining cheese mixture, remaining green onions, black olives, sour cream, green chiles and soup in a bowl and mix well. Reserve 1 cup of the sour cream mixture. Stir the chicken into the remaining sour cream mixture. Place 3 tablespoons of the chicken mixture on each tortilla and roll up. Place seam side down in a greased 9x13-inch baking dish. Spread the reserved sour cream mixture over the tortillas. Sprinkle with the reserved cheese mixture and reserved green onions. Sprinkle with paprika. Bake at 350 degrees for 45 minutes. *Yield: 6 servings.*

Carolyn Metting

Chicken Della Robbia

2 (2½- to 3-pound) chickens, cut up	4 teaspoons salt	¼ cup packed brown sugar
6 tablespoons butter	¼ cup lemon juice	1 cup walnut halves
2 medium onions, sliced	2 teaspoons MSG	4 teaspoons cornstarch
8 ounces mushrooms, sliced	½ teaspoon ground cloves	½ cup water
1 cup raisins	½ teaspoon allspice	2 cups seedless grapes
1¼ cups water	½ teaspoon ginger	2 cups orange sections
		12 maraschino cherries

Rinse the chicken and pat dry. Sauté the chicken in the butter in a Dutch oven. Add the onions, mushrooms, raisins, 1¼ cups water, salt, lemon juice, MSG, ground cloves allspice, ginger and brown sugar. Simmer, covered, until the chicken is cooked through, turning occasionally. Add the walnuts. Push the chicken to 1 side of the Dutch oven. Stir a mixture of the cornstarch and ½ cup water into the pan drippings. Cook until smooth and thickened, stirring constantly. Add the grapes, orange sections and cherries. Cook for 2 minutes or until heated through. Serve over hot buttered rice. *Yield: 8 to 12 servings.*

Penny Adams

Golfers' Chicken

8 chicken breasts	1 (12-ounce) jar apricot preserves	1 envelope onion soup mix
12 ounces Russian salad dressing		

Rinse the chicken and pat dry. Arrange the chicken to slightly overlap in a greased baking dish. Spread a mixture of the salad dressing, preserves and soup mix over the chicken. Bake at 225 degrees for 4 hours or until the chicken is cooked through. May increase the baking temperature in 25-degree increments and the baking time in 30-minute increments to adjust the baking time of the chicken to fit your golf game. May substitute your favorite chicken pieces for the chicken breasts. *Yield: 8 servings.*

Lornie Porter

Chicken Parmesan

4 skinless boneless chicken breasts
1 cup Italian salad dressing
2 (16-ounce) cans Italian stewed tomatoes
2 tablespoons cornstarch
1/2 teaspoon oregano
1/2 teaspoon basil
1/4 teaspoon hot pepper sauce
1/4 cup grated Parmesan cheese

Rinse the chicken and pat dry. Place the chicken in a shallow dish. Add the salad dressing. Marinate, covered, in the refrigerator for 1 hour. Drain the chicken, discarding the marinade. Place the chicken in a greased baking dish. Bake, covered, at 425 degrees for 15 minutes; drain. Combine the tomatoes, cornstarch, oregano, basil and pepper sauce in a saucepan. Cook until thickened, stirring constantly. Pour the sauce over the chicken. Sprinkle with the Parmesan cheese. Bake, uncovered, for 5 minutes. Garnish with chopped fresh parsley. *Yield: 4 servings.*

Betty BeDour

Easy Popover Chicken

2 1/2 to 3 pounds boneless chicken breasts
3 eggs
1 1/2 cups milk
1 1/2 cups flour
3/4 teaspoon salt
1 tablespoon vegetable oil
1 teaspoon tarragon
Mushroom Sauce

Rinse the chicken and pat dry. Arrange the chicken in a greased 9x13-inch baking pan. Combine the eggs, milk, flour and salt in a mixer bowl. Beat for 1 1/2 minutes. Stir in the vegetable oil and tarragon. Pour over the chicken. Bake at 350 degrees for 60 to 70 minutes or until cooked through. Serve with the Mushroom Sauce. *Yield: 6 to 8 servings.*

Mushroom Sauce

1 (3-ounce) can mushrooms, drained
1 tablespoon butter
1/4 cup milk
1 (10-ounce) can cream of chicken soup

Heat the mushrooms in the butter in a small saucepan. Add the milk and soup and mix well. Cook until heated through.

Nancy Compton

Chinese Walnut Chicken

2 boneless skinless chicken breasts
1/2 cup chopped walnuts
2 tablespoons vegetable oil
1/4 teaspoon salt
1/2 small onion, sliced
1 cup (scant) celery strips
2/3 cup chicken broth
1/2 teaspoon sugar
1 1/2 tablespoons cornstarch
2 tablespoons soy sauce
1/2 (8-ounce) can sliced water chestnuts, drained

Rinse the chicken and pat dry. Cut into 2-inch strips. Toast the walnuts in the vegetable oil in a skillet. Remove the walnuts to paper towels to drain. Add the chicken to the skillet and sprinkle with salt. Cook, covered, over low heat for 8 to 10 minutes or until tender, stirring frequently. Remove the chicken to a platter. Add the onion, celery and 1/4 cup of the chicken broth to the skillet. Cook, covered, for 5 minutes or until tender. Add a mixture of the sugar, cornstarch, soy sauce and the remaining chicken broth. Cook until thickened, stirring constantly. Stir in the chicken, walnuts and water chestnuts. Cook until heated through. Serve with hot rice. Yield: 2 to 4 servings.

Janice Lowell

Stir-Fried Chicken

4 boneless skinless chicken breasts
3 carrots, chopped
2 potatoes, peeled, chopped
1 tablespoon olive oil
2 teaspoons crushed garlic
1/2 small red onion, sliced, or 1 bunch green onions, chopped
1 cup sliced button mushrooms
1/2 cup marsala
2 teaspoons honey
1 tablespoon jalapeño mustard or stone-ground mustard
1/2 teaspoon salt
1/2 teaspoon pepper

Rinse the chicken and pat dry. Cut into 1/2-inch-wide strips. Boil the carrots and potatoes in water to cover in a saucepan for 4 to 5 minutes. Drain and set aside. Heat the olive oil and garlic in a sauté pan. Add the chicken. Stir-fry over medium to medium-high heat until the chicken begins to brown. Add the onion, mushrooms, carrots and potatoes and mix well. Add the wine. Reduce heat to medium-low. Simmer for 3 to 5 minutes. Stir in a mixture of the honey and mustard. Sprinkle with salt and pepper. Serve with pita bread or a salad. Yield: 4 to 6 servings.

Michael Golden

Sweet-and-Sour Chicken

1 (3-pound) chicken, cut up
Vegetable oil
1 (20-ounce) can chunk pineapple
1/2 cup green bell pepper squares
2 carrots, julienned
2 ribs celery, sliced
1/4 cup vinegar
Salt and pepper to taste

Rinse the chicken and pat dry. Brown the chicken in a small amount of vegetable oil in a skillet. Drain the pineapple, reserving the juice. Add enough water to the reserved pineapple juice to measure 3/4 cup. Add the pineapple, green pepper, carrots, celery, reserved pineapple juice mixture and vinegar to the skillet. Sprinkle with salt and pepper. Cook, covered, for 30 minutes or until the chicken is tender and cooked through. *Yield: 6 servings.*

Norah Reid

Chicken Casserole

1 (4-ounce) can mushrooms, drained
3 cups chopped cooked chicken
1 1/2 teaspoons grated onion
1 (8-ounce) can sliced water chestnuts, drained
2 cups instant rice
2 (10-ounce) cans cream of chicken soup
2 cups chicken broth
2 teaspoons lemon juice
1/2 teaspoon pepper
1 1/2 cups mayonnaise-type salad dressing
1 cup crushed potato chips

Combine the mushrooms, chicken, onion, water chestnuts, rice, chicken soup, chicken broth, lemon juice and pepper in a large bowl and mix well. Stir in the mayonnaise-type salad dressing. Spoon into a greased 9x13-inch baking dish. Sprinkle the potato chips on the top. Bake at 350 degrees for 1 hour and 10 minutes. May substitute a mixture of crumbled toasted bread, grated Parmesan cheese and melted margarine for the potato chips. *Yield: 8 to 10 servings.*

Kristi Buckner

Capilotade of Fish

1 pound cod fillets	1 teaspoon orange peel	1/4 teaspoon ginger
2 tablespoons butter	1/4 teaspoon salt	1/8 teaspoon each ground
1/2 cup bread crumbs	1/4 teaspoon nutmeg	cloves and cumin
1/4 cup chopped onion	1/4 teaspoon cinnamon	1/3 cup vinegar

Fry the fish in the butter in a skillet for 8 to 10 minutes or until the fish flakes easily. Combine the bread crumbs, onion, orange peel, salt, nutmeg, cinnamon, ginger, cloves and cumin in a bowl and mix well. Arrange half the fish in a greased baking dish. Dot with additional butter. Sprinkle with half the bread crumb mixture. Repeat the layers. Sprinkle with the vinegar. Bake, covered, at 400 degrees for 10 to 15 minutes or until heated through. *Yield: 3 to 4 servings.*

Trish Martin

Baked Whitefish Fillets

2 medium whitefish fillets	2 tablespoons butter	Paprika to taste
	Juice of 1/2 lemon	

Arrange the fish skin side down in a lightly greased shallow baking pan. Dot the fish with the butter. Drizzle the lemon juice over the fish. Sprinkle with paprika. Bake at 350 degrees for 30 minutes or until the fish flakes easily. *Yield: 2 servings.*

Kathleen Hoppenrath

Baked Stuffed Whitefish

4 cups bread cubes
¼ cup vegetable oil
2 tablespoons lemon juice
½ cup sweet pickle relish
¼ to ½ cup chopped onion
Pepper to taste
Parsley flakes to taste
1 whole whitefish, cleaned

Combine the bread cubes, vegetable oil, lemon juice, pickle relish, onion, pepper and parsley in a bowl and mix well. Cut a slit in the side of the fish, forming a pocket. Spoon the bread cube mixture into the pocket and close. Place in a greased baking pan. Bake at 350 degrees for 30 minutes or until the fish flakes easily. *Yield: 1 to 2 servings.*

Joanne Zwolinski

Boiled Whitefish

1 whole whitefish, cleaned
2 tablespoons salt
Melted butter
Pepper to taste

Cut the fish horizontally to but not through the other side. Lay the fish open. Place the fish skin side down in the bottom of a broiler pan. Sprinkle with salt. Add enough water to just cover. Cover the pan tightly. Bring just to a simmer. Simmer for 30 minutes or until the fish flakes easily. Remove the fish to a serving plate. Drizzle with a small amount of melted butter. Sprinkle with pepper. Garnish with sliced hard-cooked eggs. May make a gravy using the pan drippings to serve over the fish. This recipe originated from the recipe of Mrs. Thomas W. Ferry, 1834. *Yield: 1 to 2 servings.*

Mrs. A. W. Ferry

Mackinac Whitefish with Wine Sauce

1 1/2 pounds
whitefish fillets
Salt to taste

3 tablespoons butter
2 tablespoons flour
1 1/2 cups cream
Pepper to taste

4 egg yolks, beaten
4 egg whites, stiffly beaten
Wine Sauce

Cook the fish in salted water to just cover in a saucepan until the fish flakes easily. Remove the fish to a platter and flake. Melt the butter in a saucepan. Stir in the flour. Add the cream and salt and pepper to taste. Cook until thickened, stirring constantly. Stir a small amount of the hot mixture into the beaten egg yolks; stir into the hot mixture. Stir in the flaked fish. Fold in the stiffly beaten egg whites. Pour into a buttered fish mold. Set in a larger pan of water. Bake at 375 degrees for 40 minutes or until set. Invert onto a serving platter. Spoon a small amount of the Wine Sauce over the fish. Serve the remaining Wine Sauce on the side. *Yield: 4 to 6 servings.*

Wine Sauce

2 cups mushroom caps
1 tablespoon chopped onion

1 tablespoon butter
1/2 cup cream

2 egg yolks, beaten
Salt and pepper to taste

Sauté the mushroom caps and onion in the butter in a skillet. Stir in a mixture of the cream and egg yolks. Cook until thickened, stirring constantly. Season with salt and pepper.

Stella King

Salmon Loaf

1 (15-ounce) can salmon, flaked
1 egg, beaten
1 cup bread crumbs
Lemon juice to taste
1/2 cup chopped onion, celery and fresh parsley

Mix the salmon, egg, bread crumbs, lemon juice and onion mixture in a bowl. Press into a greased 5x9-inch loaf pan. Bake at 350 degrees or until set. *Yield: 6 to 8 servings.*

Peg Bailey

Salmon and Vegetables

1 (15-ounce) can salmon
2 large carrots, sliced, or 1 1/3 cups
6 ribs celery with leaves, sliced, or 2 cups
8 small white onions
3 cups water
1/2 teaspoon crushed thyme
1/4 teaspoon salt
1/4 teaspoon pepper
2 tablespoons minced fresh parsley
4 tablespoons butter or margarine
1/4 cup flour
1/2 cup heavy cream

Drain the salmon, reserving the liquid. Flake the salmon into chunks and set aside. Combine the carrots, celery, onions, water, thyme, salt and pepper in a saucepan. Bring to a boil. Boil for 20 to 30 minutes or until the onions are tender. Strain and reserve the vegetable stock. Combine the vegetables in a bowl with the parsley and 1 tablespoon of the butter. Return the reserved vegetable stock to the saucepan and bring to a boil.

Melt the remaining 3 tablespoons butter in a saucepan over low heat. Stir in the flour and remove from heat. Add 1 cup of the boiling reserved vegetable stock, stirring until smooth. Stir in the reserved salmon liquid. Return to low heat. Cook, covered, for 10 minutes; do not stir. Stir in the cream. Add the salmon and vegetables. Cook, covered, until heated through. *Yield: 6 servings.*

Grace O'Brien

Crab Meat Delight

2 (10-ounce) packages frozen broccoli
2 cups flaked lump crab meat
1 cup mayonnaise
2 (10-ounce) cans cream of celery soup
1 teaspoon lemon juice
1 teaspoon curry powder
3/4 cup cooking sherry
1/2 cup grated Parmesan cheese
1/2 cup bread crumbs
1/2 cup slivered almonds

Cook the broccoli in a saucepan using package directions and drain. Arrange in a greased oblong casserole. Sprinkle the crab meat over the broccoli. Combine the mayonnaise, soup, lemon juice, curry powder, cooking sherry and Parmesan cheese in a bowl and mix well. Pour over the crab meat. Sprinkle the bread crumbs and almonds over the top. Bake at 350 degrees for 25 to 30 minutes or until heated through. Garnish with strips of pimento. Yield: 6 to 8 servings.

Kathleen McDonnell

Shrimp Casserole Harpin

2 pounds fresh shrimp
Salt to taste
1/3 cup minced onion
1/3 cup minced green bell pepper
3 tablespoons vegetable oil
1 teaspoon salt
1/4 teaspoon pepper
1/4 teaspoon mace
1 tablespoon lemon juice
1 (10-ounce) can tomato soup
1 cup evaporated milk or heavy cream
1/2 cup dry sherry
1/2 cup slivered almonds
3/4 cup rice, cooked
2 tablespoons melted margarine
1/8 teaspoon paprika

Boil the shrimp in salted water to cover for 3 minutes. Remove from heat and let stand in the water until cool. Peel and devein the shrimp. Sauté the onion and green pepper in the vegetable oil in a large skillet for 3 minutes. Add 1 teaspoon salt, pepper, mace, lemon juice, soup, evaporated milk, sherry, half the almonds and rice and mix well. Spoon into a greased 2-quart casserole. Drizzle with 1 tablespoon of the margarine. Bake, covered, at 350 degrees for 20 minutes. Stir in the shrimp. Sprinkle with the remaining almonds. Drizzle with the remaining 1 tablespoon margarine. Sprinkle with the paprika. Bake for 20 minutes or until heated through. Yield: 4 to 6 servings.

Loretta Dennany

Shrimp Creole

1 large onion, sliced
1 clove of garlic, minced
4 ribs celery, chopped
2 tablespoons vegetable oil

3 1/2 cups tomatoes
Salt and pepper to taste
2 bay leaves
1 sprig of thyme
1/8 teaspoon Tabasco sauce

1/8 teaspoon Worcestershire sauce
2 pounds fresh shrimp, cooked, peeled, deveined

Sauté the onion, garlic and celery in the oil in a Dutch oven until golden brown. Add the tomatoes, salt, pepper, bay leaves, thyme, Tabasco sauce and Worcestershire sauce and mix well. Simmer for 1 hour. Let stand until cool. Chill, covered, overnight. Heat the sauce in the Dutch oven until heated through. Stir in the shrimp. Heat just until heated through. Discard the bay leaves. *Yield: 4 to 6 servings.*

Penny Adams

Curry of Shrimp

4 ounces unsalted butter, melted
1 large onion, finely chopped
3 ribs celery, finely chopped
1 small carrot, finely chopped

2 tomatoes, peeled, seeded, finely chopped
1 apple, peeled, chopped
1 tablespoon finely chopped fresh parsley
2 tablespoons flour
2 cups chicken broth or consommé, heated

1 bay leaf
1 cup white wine
Salt and pepper to taste
1 to 2 teaspoons curry powder
1 cup cream
1 1/2 pounds shrimp, cooked, peeled, deveined

Combine the butter, onion, celery, carrot, tomatoes, apple and parsley in a large saucepan. Cook over low heat until the vegetables are tender. Stir in the flour. Add the chicken broth, stirring constantly. Add the bay leaf. Cook until thickened, stirring constantly. Add the wine, salt, pepper and curry powder. Cook for 30 minutes. Stir in the cream and shrimp. Cook until heated through. Discard the bay leaf. Garnish with hard-cooked egg halves. *Yield: 4 to 6 servings.*

Helen Puttkammer

Seafood Quiche

1/2 cup chopped onion
1 cup shredded Swiss or Cheddar cheese
1 (9-inch) unbaked pie shell

1 cup evaporated milk
4 eggs
1 tablespoon sherry
2 tablespoons flour
1/4 teaspoon nutmeg

1/4 teaspoon salt
1/8 teaspoon pepper
8 ounces crab meat, peeled shrimp, scallops, haddock fillets or any combination

Sauté the onion in a nonstick skillet until transparent. Let stand until cool. Layer the onion and cheese in the pie shell. Mix the evaporated milk, eggs, sherry, flour, nutmeg, salt and pepper in a bowl. Stir in the seafood. Pour over the layers in the pie shell. Bake at 400 degrees for 10 minutes. Reduce the oven temperature to 350 degrees. Bake for 30 to 35 minutes longer or until set. May substitute milk for the evaporated milk.
Yield: 6 to 8 servings.

Trish Martin

Asparagus Casserole

2 (10-ounce) packages frozen asparagus spears, cooked, drained
1/4 cup grated onion

1 (10-ounce) package frozen small green peas, cooked, drained
1 (10-ounce) can cream of mushroom soup

1 cup shredded Cheddar cheese
Buttered bread crumbs

Arrange the asparagus in a greased baking dish. Combine the onion, green peas, soup and cheese in a bowl and mix well. Spread over the asparagus. Cover the top with the buttered bread crumbs. Bake at 350 degrees for 30 minutes or until bubbly.
Yield: 6 to 8 servings.

Thelma Solomon

Sweet Baked Beans

1 pound dried Great Northern beans or navy beans
Salt to taste
2 onions, chopped
1/2 teaspoon celery seeds
8 ounces bacon, chopped
1 cup packed brown sugar
2 tablespoons prepared mustard
1 cup chopped tomatoes

Rinse and sort the beans. Soak in water to cover in a bowl overnight and drain. Cook in salted water to cover in a saucepan until tender. Add the onions, celery seeds, bacon, brown sugar, mustard and tomatoes and mix well. Place in a greased baking dish. Bake at 350 degrees until the bacon is cooked through. *Yield: 8 to 10 servings.*

Ida Campbell

Grandma's Harvard Beets

1 (16-ounce) can beets
1/3 cup sugar
2 1/2 teaspoons cornstarch
1/4 cup vinegar
2 tablespoons butter

Drain the beets, reserving 1/4 cup of the liquid. Combine the sugar, cornstarch, vinegar and reserved beet liquid in a saucepan and mix well. Bring to a boil. Boil for 5 minutes, stirring constantly. Stir in the beets and remove from heat. Let stand for 30 minutes. Bring the beets to a boil. Stir in the butter. Serve immediately. *Yield: 4 to 6 servings.*

Trish Martin

Broccoli Stuffing Casserole

1 cup shredded sharp Cheddar cheese
2 cups milk
4 eggs, beaten
3 cups herb-seasoned croutons
¼ teaspoon salt
1 (10-ounce) package frozen chopped broccoli, thawed

Combine the cheese in the milk in a saucepan. Heat until the cheese is melted, stirring constantly. Remove from heat. Stir a small amount of the hot mixture into the beaten eggs; stir the eggs into the hot mixture. Add the croutons, salt and broccoli and mix well. Spoon into a greased 1½-quart casserole. Bake at 325 degrees for 45 minutes or until set. *Yield: 6 to 8 servings.*

Marsha Kleber

Carrot Soufflé

3 cups mashed cooked carrots
1 egg, lightly beaten
1¼ cups milk
1 tablespoon melted butter
1 tablespoon cornstarch
1 tablespoon sugar
½ teaspoon salt
⅛ teaspoon white pepper

Combine the carrots, egg, milk, butter, cornstarch, sugar, salt and white pepper in a bowl and mix well. Spoon into a buttered baking dish. Place in a larger baking dish partially filled with water. Bake at 325 degrees for 1 hour or until firm, stirring occasionally until the soufflé begins to set. *Yield: 8 servings.*

Mary Cable

Spiced Carrots

2 pounds carrots, sliced
1 (10-ounce) can tomato soup
¾ cup sugar
¼ cup vinegar
½ cup vegetable oil
⅔ cup onion, chopped
¼ teaspoon Worcestershire sauce
¼ teaspoon prepared mustard

Steam the carrots in a steamer for 7 minutes. Place in a large bowl. Combine the soup, sugar, vinegar, vegetable oil, onion, Worcestershire sauce and mustard in a bowl and mix well. Add to the carrots and mix well. Marinate, covered, in the refrigerator.
Yield: 10 to 12 servings.

Joanne Zwolinski

Eggplant Parmigiana

1 large eggplant
1 cup olive oil
1¼ cups tomato sauce
3 tablespoons grated Parmesan cheese
8 ounces mozzarella cheese, thinly sliced

Peel the eggplant and cut into thin slices. Fry in the olive oil in a skillet until brown. Remove to paper towels to drain. Alternate layers of the eggplant, tomato sauce, Parmesan cheese and mozzarella cheese in a greased casserole, ending with the mozzarella cheese. Bake at 400 degrees for 15 minutes or until cooked through. *Yield: 4 servings.*

Rosemary Brocato

Company Potatoes

6 to 7 medium white potatoes	3 tablespoons minced onion	1 teaspoon salt
1/2 cup margarine	1 1/2 cups shredded Cheddar cheese	1/2 teaspoon pepper
1 (10-ounce) can cream of chicken soup	2 cups sour cream	1 cup cornflake crumbs
		2 tablespoons melted butter

Scrub and rinse the potatoes. Boil the unpeeled potatoes in water to cover until tender. Drain and let stand until cool. Peel the cooled potatoes and medium grate into a large bowl. Heat the margarine and soup in a saucepan. Stir in the onion, Cheddar cheese, sour cream, salt and pepper. Add to the potatoes and mix well. Pour into a greased 9x11-inch glass baking dish. Sprinkle with a mixture of the cornflakes and melted butter. Chill overnight. Bake at 350 degrees for 45 to 60 minutes or until bubbly. *Yield: 8 to 10 servings.*

Carl Nold

Potatoes Deluxe

5 cups frozen hash brown potatoes, thawed	1 cup sour cream	1 teaspoon salt
2 cups cottage cheese	1/2 cup chopped onion	1 teaspoon garlic salt (optional)
	1 cup shredded Cheddar cheese	

Combine the potatoes, cottage cheese, sour cream, onion, Cheddar cheese, salt and garlic salt in a large bowl and mix well. Spoon into a large baking dish. Bake at 350 degrees for 1 hour. *Yield: 4 to 6 servings.*

Meg Brown

Hot German Potato Salad

3 medium potatoes
3 slices bacon, chopped
2 tablespoons flour

¼ to ½ cup vinegar
1 cup water

1 medium onion, chopped
1 teaspoon sugar
Salt and pepper to taste

Scrub and rinse the potatoes. Boil in water to cover in a saucepan until tender and drain. Let stand until cool. Fry the bacon in a skillet until crisp. Remove the bacon to a bowl using a slotted spoon. Stir the flour into the bacon drippings in the skillet. Stir in the vinegar and water. Cook until thickened, stirring constantly. Peel the cooled potatoes and slice into a bowl. Add the onion and sugar and mix well. Add to the gravy in the skillet. Heat over low heat until the potatoes are heated through. Season with salt and pepper. Stir in the bacon. Spoon into a serving bowl. Garnish with hard-cooked eggs. *Yield: 4 to 6 servings.*

Maria Moeller

Deep-Fried Potato Balls

1 cup mashed cooked potatoes
1 cup flour

1 teaspoon baking powde
1 teaspoon salt
1 egg, beaten

5 tablespoons milk
Vegetable oil for deep-frying

Combine the potatoes, flour, baking powder, salt, egg and milk in a bowl and mix well. Heat the vegetable oil in a deep fryer to 375 degrees. Drop the batter by tablespoonfuls into the hot oil. Deep-fry until golden brown. Drain on paper towels. Serve hot. *Yield: 4 to 5 servings.*

Anna Lasley

Stampede Potato Pudding

8 ounces bacon, chopped
8 large potatoes, grated
1 large onion, grated
2 eggs, beaten
1/8 teaspoon sugar
Salt to taste

Fry the bacon in a skillet until crisp. Remove from heat. Stir in the potatoes and onion. Cool slightly. Stir in the eggs, sugar and salt. Spoon into a baking dish. Bake at 350 degrees for 1 hour. *Yield: 10 to 12 servings.*

Gracie Koerbel

Potato Pancakes

8 to 10 potatoes, peeled, grated
1/2 cup baking mix
1/4 cup half-and-half
2 eggs, beaten
1 small onion, grated
1 teaspoon salt
1/2 teaspoon pepper

Combine the potatoes, baking mix, half-and-half, eggs, onion, salt and pepper in a bowl and mix well. Drop by tablespoonfuls onto a preheated greased griddle. Flatten with the back of a spoon. Bake for 5 minutes on each side or until golden brown. *Yield: 4 to 6 servings.*

Mary Rogers

Spinach and Cheese Tart

1 pound fresh spinach, cooked
1 cup cottage cheese
3 tablespoons grated Parmesan cheese
Salt and pepper to taste
1 egg, lightly beaten
2 green onions, chopped

Drain the spinach well, squeezing out any excess moisture. Combine the spinach, cottage cheese, Parmesan cheese, salt and pepper in a bowl and mix well. Add the beaten egg and green onions and mix well. Spread in a greased 8-inch pie plate. Bake at 350 degrees for 30 minutes or until set. Let stand for 10 to 15 minutes before serving. May substitute one 10-ounce package frozen chopped spinach for the fresh spinach. *Yield: 6 to 8 servings.*

Anne St. Onge

Sausage Ball-Stuffed Squash

2 medium acorn squash
1 pound bulk pork
  sausage

2 cups sweetened
  applesauce

Cinnamon to taste
Salt to taste

Cut the squash into halves lengthwise and remove the seeds. Place cut side down in a greased shallow baking pan. Bake at 350 degrees for 35 to 40 minutes or just until tender. Shape the sausage into small balls. Cook in a skillet over low heat for 15 minutes or until brown and cooked through; drain. Add a mixture of the applesauce and cinnamon. Simmer, covered, for 15 minutes. Turn the squash cut side up in the baking pan and sprinkle with salt. Fill with the sausage ball mixture. Bake for 20 minutes or until the squash is tender. *Yield: 4 servings.*

Nettie Hildreth

Apple Mallow Yam Bake

2 apples, sliced
1/3 cup chopped pecans
  (optional)
1/2 teaspoon cinnamon

1/2 cup packed brown
  sugar

2 (17-ounce) cans
  yams, drained
1/4 cup margarine
Marshmallows

Combine the apples, pecans, cinnamon and brown sugar in a bowl and toss to coat well. Spoon into a 1 1/2-quart baking dish. Layer the yams over the apple mixture. Dot with the margarine. Bake at 350 degrees for 35 to 40 minutes. Sprinkle with marshmallows. Bake until the marshmallows are light brown. *Yield: 6 to 8 servings.*

Elizabeth Sieffert

Zucchini with Walnuts

2 tablespoons olive oil
2 zucchini, cut into
½-inch slices
1 red onion, thinly sliced
½ cup chopped walnuts or cashews
½ teaspoon tarragon
Salt and pepper to taste
1 tablespoon thawed frozen orange juice concentrate

Heat the olive oil in a large skillet. Add the zucchini and onion. Sauté over high heat just until tender. Add the walnuts. Sauté for 1 to 2 minutes or until the vegetables begin to brown. Stir in the tarragon, salt, pepper and orange juice concentrate. Cook for 1 to 2 minutes. Serve immediately with broiled whitefish or chicken. *Yield: 4 to 6 servings.*

Candi Dunnigan

Vegetables au Gratin

¾ cup coarsely chopped green bell pepper
¼ cup melted butter
¼ cup flour
⅔ cup milk
¾ teaspoon salt
¼ teaspoon sugar
⅛ teaspoon pepper
⅛ teaspoon basil
⅛ teaspoon oregano
½ cup shredded Cheddar cheese
1 cup drained tomatoes
1 (10-ounce) package frozen corn, thawed
1 (16-ounce) jar whole sweet onions, rinsed, drained
½ cup shredded Cheddar cheese

Sauté the green pepper in the melted butter in a saucepan until slightly tender. Stir in the flour. Add the milk, salt, sugar, pepper, basil and oregano. Cook until thickened, stirring constantly. Remove from heat. Stir in ½ cup Cheddar cheese. Add the tomatoes, corn and drained onions. Spoon into a greased casserole. Sprinkle with ½ cup Cheddar cheese. Bake at 350 degrees for 50 minutes. May prepare this recipe ahead of time and chill until ready to bake. *Yield: 6 servings.*

Sally Dufina

Baked Noodle Casserole

8 ounces very fine egg noodles, cooked, drained
1 cup creamed cottage cheese
1/4 cup finely minced onion
1 cup sour cream
1 clove of garlic, finely minced
2 teaspoons Worcestershire sauce
2 tablespoons prepared horseradish
2 teaspoons salt
1/8 teaspoon Tabasco sauce
1/2 cup grated Parmesan cheese

Combine the noodles, cottage cheese, onion, sour cream, garlic, Worcestershire sauce, horseradish, salt, Tabasco sauce and Parmesan cheese in a large bowl and mix well. Spoon into a buttered casserole. Bake, covered, at 350 degrees for 45 minutes. Remove the cover and sprinkle with additional Parmesan cheese. Broil until the top is golden brown. *Yield: 6 servings.*

Mary Cable

Rice and Cheese Soufflé

2 cups cooked rice
2 to 4 ounces Cheddar cheese, shredded
1 tablespoon melted butter
2 egg yolks, beaten
1 cup milk
1/2 teaspoon salt
1/8 teaspoon paprika
2 egg whites, stiffly beaten

Combine the rice, cheese, butter, egg yolks, milk, salt and paprika in a bowl and mix well. Fold in the stiffly beaten egg whites. Spoon into a greased baking dish. Bake at 350 degrees for 25 minutes or until set. *Yield: 4 to 6 servings.*

Mary Benjamin

Conserve for Meat

1 orange
4 cups cranberries
2 cups seedless raisins
1 cup shredded pineapple
1 cup chopped pecans
2 cups packed brown sugar
4 ounces brandy

Peel the orange and grate the zest. Mince the orange pulp, discarding the seeds. Cook the cranberries in water to cover in a saucepan until the cranberries pop. Add the orange zest, orange pulp, raisins, pineapple, pecans and brown sugar. Cook until thickened, stirring occasionally. Spoon into a serving dish. Pour the brandy over the top. May heat the brandy, ignite and pour flaming over the conserve. *Yield: 12 to 15 servings.*

Sara Chambers

Pleasants

1 to 2 cups flour
1 teaspoon salt
2 teaspoons baking powder
Milk or water
Chicken, beef, venison or rabbit broth

Mix the flour, salt and baking powder in a bowl. Stir in just enough milk to make a soft dough; do not knead. Roll into a thin rectangle on a lightly floured surface. Cut into squares. Drop into hot boiling chicken broth in a large saucepan. Cook, covered, for 20 minutes. Serve hot. This old French dish is excellent served with stews.
Yield: 4 to 6 servings.

Stella King

Barbecue Sauce

2 medium onions, chopped
1 cup vinegar
1 (14-ounce) bottle catsup
2 cups vegetable oil or margarine
1 (10-ounce) bottle Worcestershire sauce
Juice and peel of 2 lemons
1 tablespoon chili powder
2 teaspoons salt
1/8 teaspoon cayenne or black pepper

Bring the onions to a boil in the vinegar in a saucepan. Boil for 5 minutes. Add the catsup, vegetable oil, Worcestershire sauce, lemon juice, lemon peel, chili powder, salt and cayenne and mix well. Return to a boil and reduce heat. Simmer for 10 minutes. Store, covered, in the refrigerator. Use on ribs or chicken or on all kinds of meat. *Yield: 6 to 7 cups.*

Sara Chambers

Sweet-and-Sour Sauce

6 cloves of garlic, crushed
1 medium onion, finely chopped
1 teaspoon ground, shaved or minced fresh ginger
2 tablespoons canola oil
2 tablespoons red wine or white vinegar
2 ounces mild green chiles, chopped
3 cups undrained stewed tomatoes, chopped
1 cup crushed pineapple
1 tablespoon lemon juice
1 tablespoon lime juice
1/4 cup sugar
1 tablespoon soy sauce
2 teaspoons salt
1 teaspoon pepper

Simmer the garlic, onion and ginger in the canola oil in a saucepan over medium heat for 3 minutes. Stir in the vinegar carefully. Add the green chiles, tomatoes, pineapple, lemon juice, lime juice, sugar, soy sauce, salt and pepper and mix well. Reduce heat to low. Simmer for 15 minutes, stirring occasionally. Serve with fresh sautéed vegetables over hot rice. This sauce is also good with chicken, fish or sautéed shrimp. *Yield: 4 to 5 cups.*

Michael Golden

Fresh Tomato Sauce

1/4 cup olive oil
2 tablespoons fresh lemon juice
2 teaspoons lemon zest
3/4 teaspoon salt

3/4 teaspoon cracked pepper
2 pounds plum tomatoes, chopped
1/2 bunch fresh parsley, coarsely chopped

3 tablespoons drained capers
1 red onion, chopped
Coarsely chopped walnuts (optional)

Combine the olive oil, lemon juice, lemon zest, salt and pepper in a large bowl. Stir in the tomatoes, parsley, capers and onion. Marinate, covered, in the refrigerator for 2 hours or longer. Stir in the walnuts just before serving. Serve over cooked pasta or grilled French bread. *Yield: 4 to 6 servings.*

Betty BeDour

Tomato Sauce

1 small onion, chopped
1/2 rib celery, finely chopped
1 clove of garlic, minced
1 teaspoon parsley, minced

3 tablespoons olive oil
1 (28-ounce) can Italian tomatoes
1 (11-ounce) can tomato purée

1/2 teaspoon salt
1/2 teaspoon pepper
1/2 teaspoon minced fresh basil
1/2 teaspoon oregano
1 bay leaf

Sauté the onion, celery, garlic and parsley in the olive oil in a saucepan until light brown. Add the tomatoes, tomato purée, salt and pepper and mix well. Simmer for 45 minutes. Stir in the basil, oregano and bay leaf. Cook for 10 minutes longer. Discard the bay leaf before serving. Serve over spaghetti or macaroni. May substitute 1/4 cup butter for the olive oil. *Yield: 4 to 6 servings.*

Rosemary Brocato

Tasteful Extras

Breads

Neapolitan or Buttermilk Biscuits

3/4 cup packed brown sugar	1 cup buttermilk or sour milk	1/2 teaspoon baking soda
1/2 cup shortening	2 3/4 cups flour	1/2 teaspoon nutmeg
1 egg	2 teaspoons baking powder	1/2 cup raisins

Beat the brown sugar and shortening in a mixer bowl until creamy. Add the egg, beating until blended. Beat in the buttermilk. Stir in the flour, baking powder, baking soda and nutmeg. Add the raisins and mix well. Pat the dough on a lightly floured surface; cut with a floured biscuit cutter. Arrange on a baking sheet. Bake at 450 degrees for 15 minutes. Yield: 12 to 15 biscuits.

Mable Breuckman

Cheese Biscuits

2 cups sifted flour	3 tablespoons (rounded) shortening	8 ounces Cheddar cheese
4 teaspoons baking powder	2/3 cup milk	Milk to taste or melted butter
1 teaspoon salt	1/2 cup butter or margarine, softened	Paprika to taste

Combine the flour, baking powder and salt in a bowl and mix well. Cut in the shortening until crumbly. Stir in 2/3 cup milk. Divide the dough into 2 portions. Pat each portion 1/4 inch thick on a lightly floured surface. Spread each portion with a mixture of the butter and cheese. Roll as for a jelly roll; slice. Arrange cut side up on a baking sheet. Brush with milk to taste or butter; sprinkle with paprika. Bake at 400 degrees for 10 to 15 minutes or until brown. Serve hot. Roll the dough thinner and cut into smaller slices if the biscuits are to be used for hors d'oeuvre. Yield: 9 to 12 biscuits.

Grandma's Kitchen

Scottish Scones

2 1/2 cups flour
2/3 cup packed brown sugar
4 teaspoons baking powder

1/2 cup shortening
1/2 cup butter or margarine, softened
2 cups rolled oats or quick-cooking oats
2/3 cup raisins

2/3 cup milk
1 tablespoon melted butter
2 tablespoons sugar
1/2 teaspoon cinnamon

Combine the flour, brown sugar and baking powder in a bowl and mix well. Cut in the shortening and butter until crumbly. Stir in the oats, raisins and milk. Divide the dough into 2 portions and knead lightly. Shape each portion into a 6- or 7-inch circle on a lightly floured surface. Brush with butter; sprinkle with sugar and cinnamon. Cut each circle into 8 wedges. Arrange on a greased baking sheet. Bake at 375 degrees for 12 to 15 minutes. Serve hot or cold. *Yield: 16 servings.*

Trish Martin

Aunt Leila's Coffee Cakes

4 1/2 cups flour
2 1/4 cups sugar
3 tablespoons baking powder
1/8 teaspoon salt

3/4 cup shortening
1 1/2 cups milk
3 eggs
1 tablespoon vanilla extract
1 cup packed brown sugar

1/4 cup flour
1/4 cup melted butter
2 tablespoons cinnamon
1 cup chopped nuts (optional)

Grease and flour 2 tube pans. Combine 4 1/2 cups flour, sugar, baking powder and salt in a bowl and mix well. Cut in the shortening until crumbly. Add the milk, eggs and vanilla and mix well. Combine the brown sugar, 1/4 cup flour, butter and cinnamon in a bowl and mix well. Layer the batter and brown sugar mixture 1/4 at a time in each of the prepared pans. Bake at 350 degrees for 35 minutes or until the coffee cakes test done. *Yield: 32 servings.*

Alice Martin

Easy Coffee Cake

2 cups flour
1 cup sugar
1/8 teaspoon salt

2 teaspoons baking
powder
1 cup milk

1 egg, beaten
Cinnamon and sugar
to taste

Combine the flour, sugar, salt and baking powder in a bowl and mix well. Stir in the milk and egg. Spoon into an ungreased round baking dish. Sprinkle with cinnamon and sugar. Bake at 350 degrees until brown. *Yield: 8 servings.*

Mary Benjamin

Frozen Biscuit Coffee Cake

18 frozen dinner
rolls

1 (4-ounce) package
butterscotch pudding and
pie filling mix

1/2 cup margarine
1/2 cup packed brown
sugar

Arrange the rolls in a greased bundt pan or angel food cake pan. Sprinkle with the pudding mix. Bring the margarine and brown sugar to a boil in a saucepan. Cook until the brown sugar dissolves, stirring constantly. Spoon around the rolls. Let stand, covered with waxed paper, for 8 to 10 hours. Bake at 350 degrees for 25 to 30 minutes or until the coffee cake tests done. *Yield: 16 servings.*

Kristi Buckner

Vienna Coffee Cake

1 1/2 cups plus 2 tablespoons cake flour
2 2/3 teaspoons baking powder
1/4 teaspoon salt
1 cup sugar
1/4 cup butter, softened
2 eggs
1/2 cup milk
1 tablespoon melted butter
2 tablespoons sugar
1/2 cup chopped walnuts

Sift the cake flour, baking powder and salt into a bowl and mix well. Beat 1 cup sugar and butter in a mixer bowl until creamy, scraping the bowl occasionally. Add the eggs 1 at a time, beating until light and fluffy after each addition. Add the dry ingredients alternately with the milk, beginning with the dry ingredients. Spoon into a baking pan. Drizzle with the melted butter. Sprinkle with 2 tablespoons sugar and the walnuts. Bake at 350 degrees for 45 minutes. *Yield: 10 servings.*

Grand Hotel

Southern Spoon Bread

3 cups milk
1/2 cup white cornmeal
2 egg yolks, lightly beaten
2 tablespoons butter or margarine
1 teaspoon salt
1/2 teaspoon baking powder
2 egg whites, stiffly beaten

Scald 1 1/2 cups of the milk in a saucepan. Stir 1/2 cup of the remaining milk into the cornmeal in a bowl. Stir the cornmeal mixture into the scalded milk. Cook over low heat for 5 minutes or until of the consistency of mush, stirring occasionally. Stir in a mixture of the remaining 1 cup milk, egg yolks, butter, salt and baking powder. Cook until the butter melts, stirring constantly. Fold in the stiffly beaten egg whites. Spoon into a greased 1 1/2-quart baking dish. Bake at 350 degrees for 1 hour and 10 minutes or until set.
Yield: 4 to 6 servings.

Stella King

Raised Cornmeal Muffins

1 cake yeast or 1 envelope dry yeast	1/2 cup sugar	2 cups milk, scalded
1/2 cup lukewarm water	1/2 cup shortening	2 eggs
2 cups yellow cornmeal	1 tablespoon salt	3 cups flour
		Melted butter

Soften the yeast in the lukewarm water and mix well. Combine the cornmeal, sugar, shortening and salt in a bowl. Pour the milk over the cornmeal mixture and mix well. Let stand until lukewarm. Beat in the eggs and 2/3 of the flour. Stir in the yeast mixture. Add just enough of the remaining flour to make a heavy batter and mix well. Let rise, covered, for 1 hour or until doubled in bulk. Stir the dough down. Fill greased muffin cups 2/3 full. Let rise in a warm place until doubled in bulk. Bake at 400 degrees for 15 to 20 minutes or until brown. Brush lightly with butter. Serve warm. *Yield: 20 muffins.*

Jessie Joy

Apricot Bread

1 cup chopped dried apricots	1 cup sugar	1/4 cup shortening
3/4 cup orange juice	1 1/2 teaspoons baking powder	1 egg, beaten
2 cups flour	1 teaspoon salt	1/2 cup chopped nuts (optional)
	1/2 teaspoon baking soda	

Soak the apricots in the orange juice in a bowl for 30 minutes. Combine the flour, sugar, baking powder, salt and baking soda in a bowl and mix well. Cut in the shortening until crumbly. Add the apricot mixture and egg, stirring just until moistened. May add additional orange juice if needed for the desired consistency. Fold in the nuts. Spoon into a greased loaf pan. Bake at 350 degrees for 1 hour. Cool in the pan on a wire rack for 20 minutes. Invert onto a wire rack to cool completely. *Yield: 1 loaf.*

Carol Morlock

Ray's Banana Bread

2 cups sugar	6 large ripe bananas,	2 teaspoons salt
1 cup vegetable oil	mashed	2 teaspoons baking soda
4 eggs	2½ cups flour	Chopped nuts to taste

Beat the sugar, oil, eggs and bananas in a mixer bowl until mixed. Stir in a mixture of the flour, salt and baking soda. Fold in the nuts. Spoon into a greased and floured bundt pan. Bake at 350 degrees for 1 hour or until the bread tests done. May bake in greased and floured loaf pans for 45 minutes. *Yield: 16 servings.*

Marilyn Wilkins

Banana Luncheon Bread

2 cups flour	½ teaspoon baking soda	2 eggs
1 teaspoon salt	1 cup sugar	1 cup mashed bananas
1 teaspoon baking powder	½ cup shortening	½ cup chopped nuts

Sift the flour, salt, baking powder and baking soda into a bowl and mix well. Beat the sugar and shortening in a mixer bowl until creamy. Add the eggs 1 at a time, beating well after each addition. Stir in the bananas. Add the dry ingredients and mix well. Fold in the nuts. Spoon into a greased 5x9-inch loaf pan. Push the batter up in the corners, leaving the center slightly hollow. Bake at 350 degrees for 60 to 70 minutes or until the loaf tests done. Allow the batter to stand at room temperature for 20 minutes before baking for a well-rounded loaf. *Yield: 1 loaf.*

Ruby Bloswick

Bran Bread

3 cups sour milk or buttermilk
2 teaspoons baking soda
4 cups flour

2 teaspoons salt
3 cups 40% Bran Flakes
1 cup sugar

2 eggs, beaten
1/2 cup molasses
1 cup raisins
1 cup chopped nuts

Combine the sour milk and baking soda in a bowl and mix well. Sift the flour and salt together. Combine the Bran Flakes, sugar and eggs in a bowl and mix well. Add the sour milk mixture alternately with the flour mixture, mixing well after each addition. Add the molasses and mix well. Stir in the raisins and nuts. Spoon into 2 loaf pans. Bake at 350 degrees for 1 hour. *Yield: 2 loaves.*

Ethel Ryba

Irish Brown Bread

2 cups whole wheat flour
1/2 cup all-purpose flour
1 tablespoon baking powder

1 tablespoon baking soda
1 1/2 cups buttermilk

1/4 to 2/3 cup dark molasses
1/4 cup vegetable oil
1/4 cup honey

Combine the whole wheat flour, all-purpose flour, baking powder and baking soda in a bowl and mix well. Stir in the buttermilk, molasses, oil and honey. Spoon into a greased loaf pan. Bake at 350 degrees for 40 to 50 minutes or until the loaf tests done. *Yield: 1 loaf.*

Candi Dunnigan

Cinnamon Bread

1/2 cup sugar
2 teaspoons cinnamon
4 cups flour
2 teaspoons baking soda
2 teaspoons baking powder
1 teaspoon salt
2 cups sugar
1 cup shortening
4 eggs
2 teaspoons vanilla extract
2 cups buttermilk

Combine 1/2 cup sugar and cinnamon in a bowl and mix well. Combine the flour, baking soda, baking powder and salt in a bowl and mix well. Beat 2 cups sugar and shortening in a mixer bowl until creamy. Add the eggs and vanilla, beating until blended. Add the dry ingredients alternately with the buttermilk, beating well after each addition. Spoon 1/2 of the batter into 2 greased 5x9-inch loaf pans. Sprinkle with 1/2 of the sugar and cinnamon mixture. Spread with the remaining batter; sprinkle with the remaining sugar and cinnamon mixture. Swirl through batter with a knife. Bake at 350 degrees for 1 hour or until the loaves test done. May bake in 4 greased miniature loaf pans. *Yield: 2 loaves.*

Meg Brown

Cranberry Bread

2 cups sifted flour
1 cup sugar
1 1/2 teaspoons baking soda
1/2 teaspoon salt
Juice of 1 orange
2 tablespoons melted margarine or shortening
Boiling water
1 egg, beaten
1 cup fresh cranberries, cut into halves or quarters
1/3 cup chopped pecans

Combine the flour, sugar, baking soda and salt in a bowl and mix well. Combine the orange juice and margarine in a measuring cup and mix well. Add enough boiling water to measure 3/4 cup and mix well. Stir into the flour mixture. Add the egg and mix well. Fold in the cranberries and pecans. Spoon into a greased 5x9-inch loaf pan. Bake at 325 degrees for 1 hour. May substitute canned cranberries for the fresh cranberries, reducing the amount of boiling water added to measure to 1/2 cup. Great toasted and served with coffee. *Yield: 1 loaf.*

Grace O'Brien

Date-Nut Bread

1 cup chopped dates
1 cup packed brown sugar
3 tablespoons melted butter
1 cup boiling water
1 teaspoon baking soda
1/2 teaspoon vanilla extract
2 eggs, beaten
2 cups flour
1/2 cup chopped nuts

Combine the dates, brown sugar and butter in a bowl and mix well. Pour a mixture of the boiling water and baking soda over the top and mix well. Let stand until cool. Stir in the vanilla and eggs. Add the flour gradually and mix well. Stir in the nuts. Spoon into a 5x9-inch loaf pan. Bake at 350 degrees for 1 hour or until the loaf tests done. *Yield: 1 loaf.*

Esther L. Wightman

Nut Bread

2 cups sifted flour
1/2 teaspoon baking powder
1 teaspoon baking soda
1/4 teaspoon salt
1 cup packed brown sugar
1 egg, beaten
1 cup sour milk
1/2 cup chopped nuts

Sift the flour, baking powder, baking soda and salt into a bowl and mix well. Beat the brown sugar and egg in a mixer bowl until blended. Add the sour milk, beating until blended. Stir in the dry ingredients. Fold in the nuts. Spoon into a loaf pan. Bake at 350 degrees for 1 hour or until the loaf tests done. May use sweet milk instead of sour milk, omitting the baking soda and increasing the baking powder to 1 tablespoon. *Yield: 1 loaf.*

Mary McIntyre

Orange Bread

3 cups flour
1 cup sugar
3/4 teaspoon salt
4 teaspoons baking powder
1 cup orange juice
1/3 cup melted shortening
1/4 cup grated orange peel
1 egg, beaten

Sift the flour, sugar, salt and baking powder into a bowl and mix well. Combine the orange juice, shortening, orange peel and egg in a bowl and mix well. Add to the flour mixture, stirring just until moistened. Spoon into a greased loaf pan. Bake at 250 degrees for 1 hour or until the loaf tests done. *Yield: 1 loaf.*

Aleda Schmidt

Orange Quick Bread

Grated peel and juice of 1 medium orange
1 cup raisins
Boiling water
2 tablespoons melted shortening
1 teaspoon vanilla extract
1 egg, beaten
2 cups flour, sifted
1 cup sugar
1 teaspoon baking powder
1/2 teaspoon baking soda
1/4 teaspoon salt

Combine the orange peel and raisins in a bowl and mix well. Pour the orange juice into a measuring cup. Add enough boiling water to measure 1 cup and mix well. Pour over the raisin mixture. Stir in the shortening, vanilla and egg. Add a mixture of the flour, sugar, baking powder, baking soda and salt and mix well. Spoon into a waxed-paper-lined 5x9-inch loaf pan. Bake at 350 degrees for 1 hour or until the loaf tests done. *Yield: 1 loaf.*

Mary Kate McGreevy

Prune Bread

1 pound prunes
2 cups sugar
3/4 cup shortening
1 teaspoon cinnamon
1 teaspoon salt
1/2 teaspoon nutmeg
1/4 teaspoon ground cloves
2 eggs, beaten
4 cups flour, sifted
2 tablespoons baking cocoa
2 teaspoons baking soda

Soak the prunes in a generous amount of water in a bowl for 8 to 10 hours. Drain, reserving 2 cups of the liquid. Pit and chop the prunes. Combine the prunes, 2 cups reserved liquid, sugar, shortening, cinnamon, salt, nutmeg and cloves in a saucepan and mix well. Cook for 5 minutes, stirring frequently. Let stand until cool. Add the eggs and mix well. Stir in a sifted mixture of the flour, baking cocoa and baking soda. Spoon into 2 greased 5x9-inch loaf pans. Bake at 350 degrees for 1 hour or until the loaves test done. Cool on a wire rack. Mellow, wrapped, for 2 days before serving. *Yield: 2 loaves.*

Hannabass Girls

Pumpkin Bread

3 1/3 cups flour
2 teaspoons baking soda
2 teaspoons nutmeg
2 teaspoons cinnamon
1 1/2 teaspoons salt
1 teaspoon allspice
1 1/2 cups sugar
1 1/2 cups packed brown sugar
1 cup shortening or vegetable oil
4 eggs
2/3 cup buttermilk or sour milk
2 cups pumpkin
2 cups chopped walnuts

Combine the flour, baking soda, nutmeg, cinnamon, salt and allspice in a bowl and mix well. Beat the sugar, brown sugar and shortening in a mixer bowl until creamy. Add the eggs, beating until blended. Add the dry ingredients alternately with the buttermilk, mixing well after each addition. Stir in the pumpkin and walnuts. Spoon into 3 greased miniature loaf pans or 2 greased 5x9-inch loaf pans. Bake at 350 degrees for 1 hour or until the loaves test done. *Yield: 3 miniature loaves.*

Carmen Golden

Zucchini Bread

3 cups flour
1 to 3 teaspoons cinnamon
1 teaspoon baking soda
1 teaspoon salt
1/4 teaspoon baking powder
2 cups sugar
1 cup vegetable oil
3 eggs
1 tablespoon vanilla extract
2 cups ground zucchini, drained
1/2 cup ground nuts

Combine the flour, cinnamon, baking soda, salt and baking powder in a bowl and mix well. Beat the sugar, oil and eggs in a mixer bowl until blended. Stir in the vanilla and zucchini. Add the dry ingredients and mix well. Stir in the nuts. Spoon into 2 greased loaf pans. Bake at 350 degrees for 1 hour or until the loaves test done. *Yield: 2 loaves.*

Peg Clark

Bran Muffins

2 cups oat bran
1 (16-ounce) can whole cranberry sauce
2 tablespoons corn oil
2 teaspoons (heaping) baking powder
2 egg whites
1/2 cup chopped walnuts

Combine the oat bran, cranberry sauce, corn oil, baking powder and egg whites in a bowl, stirring just until moistened. Fold in the walnuts. Spoon into muffin cups sprayed with nonstick cooking spray. Bake at 425 degrees for 15 to 17 minutes or until the muffins test done. *Yield: 12 muffins.*

Carmen Golden

Float-Away Tea Cake Muffins

2 cups cake flour	1 teaspoon salt	1/2 cup shortening
1 1/4 cups sugar	2/3 cup milk, at room temperature	2 eggs, at room temperature
2 teaspoons baking powder		1 teaspoon vanilla extract

Sift the cake flour, sugar, baking powder and salt into a mixer bowl and mix well. Add the milk and shortening. Beat for 2 minutes or until blended. Add the eggs and vanilla. Beat for 2 minutes longer, scraping the bowl occasionally. Fill lightly greased muffins cups 1/3 to 1/2 full. Bake at 375 degrees for 20 to 25 minutes or until the muffins test done. May substitute butter or margarine for the shortening, decreasing the milk to 1/2 cup. *Yield: 18 muffins.*

Helen Dufina

Zucchini Muffins

3 cups flour	2 cups sugar	1/2 teaspoon vanilla extract
1 teaspoon baking powder	4 eggs, at room temperature	1 cup chopped walnuts
1 teaspoon baking soda	1 cup vegetable oil	1 cup raisins
1 teaspoon salt	2 cups grated unpeeled zucchini	
1 teaspoon cinnamon		

Sift the flour, baking powder, baking soda, salt and cinnamon into a bowl and mix well. Combine the sugar and eggs in a mixer bowl. Beat at medium speed for 2 minutes. Add the oil in a fine stream, beating constantly for 2 to 3 minutes. Add the zucchini and vanilla and mix well. Stir in the walnuts and raisins. Add the dry ingredients, mixing just until moistened. Fill greased or paper-lined muffin cups 2/3 full. Bake at 350 degrees for 25 minutes or until the muffins test done. Cool in the cups for 10 minutes. Invert onto a wire rack to cool completely. *Yield: 12 to 15 muffins.*

Debbie Fisher

Poppy Seed Muffins

1 (2-layer) package yellow cake mix
1 cup hot water
1/2 cup vegetable oil
1 (4-ounce) package toasted coconut instant pudding mix
4 eggs
3 tablespoons poppy seeds

Combine the cake mix, hot water, oil, pudding mix, eggs and poppy seeds in a bowl and mix just until moistened. Spoon into muffin cups. Bake at 350 degrees for 20 to 25 minutes or until the muffins test done. May bake in 2 loaf pans for 40 to 50 minutes or until the loaves test done. *Yield: 12 to 18 muffins.*

Nancy Compton

Coffee-Can Bread

1 envelope dry yeast
1/2 cup lukewarm water
1 tablespoon sugar
1/8 teaspoon ginger
2 tablespoons sugar
1 teaspoon salt
1 (12-ounce) can evaporated milk
2 tablespoons vegetable oil
4 to 4 1/2 cups unbleached flour
Melted butter or margarine

Dissolve the yeast in the lukewarm water in a mixer bowl and mix well. Stir in 1 tablespoon sugar and ginger. Let stand in a warm place for 15 minutes or until bubbly. Stir in the 2 tablespoons sugar, salt, evaporated milk and oil. Add 3 cups of the flour 1 cup at a time, beating at low speed constantly. Beat in by hand just enough of the remaining 1 1/2 cups flour to make a heavy dough. Spoon into 2 greased 1-pound coffee cans. Cover with greased plastic can lids. May freeze at this point if desired.

    Let stand in a warm place for 1 hour or until dough pops off the lids. Bake at 350 degrees for 40 to 45 minutes. Brush tops with butter. Cool for 5 to 10 minutes in coffee cans on a wire rack. Run a knife around the edge of the bread. Slide the bread out of the cans. Cool on a wire rack in an upright position. If frozen, let the cans stand at room temperature for 4 to 5 hours or until the dough pops off the lids. For whole wheat bread, substitute 1 1/2 cups whole wheat flour and 3 cups all-purpose flour for the unbleached flour and substitute 3 tablespoons honey for the sugar. *Yield: 2 loaves.*

Lornie Porter

Dilly Bread

1 envelope dry yeast	1 tablespoon instant onion flakes	1/4 teaspoon baking soda
1/4 cup lukewarm water		1 egg
1 cup cottage cheese, heated	1 tablespoon butter	2 1/4 to 2 1/2 cups flour
	2 teaspoons dillseeds	Melted butter
2 tablespoons sugar	1 teaspoon salt	Salt to taste

Dissolve the yeast in the lukewarm water in a bowl. Stir in the cottage cheese, sugar, onion flakes, 1 tablespoon butter, dillseeds, 1 teaspoon salt, baking soda and egg. Add just enough flour to make a stiff dough and mix well. Let rise, covered, for 50 to 60 minutes or until doubled in bulk. Stir the dough down. Shape into a loaf in a greased loaf pan. Let rise for 40 minutes or until light. Bake at 350 degrees for 40 to 50 minutes or until the loaf tests done. Brush with melted butter; sprinkle with salt to taste. *Yield: 1 loaf.*

Joanne Zwolinski

Egg Bread

2 (1-ounce) cakes yeast	1 1/2 cups milk, scalded	1 1/2 teaspoons salt
1/2 cup lukewarm water	1/4 cup butter	3 eggs
1 teaspoon sugar	1/2 cup sugar	7 1/2 cups sifted flour

Dissolve the yeast in the lukewarm water in a bowl. Stir in 1 teaspoon sugar. Let stand for 5 minutes. Combine the milk, butter, 1/2 cup sugar and salt in a mixer bowl and mix well. Cool to lukewarm. Stir in the yeast mixture and eggs. Beat until smooth, scraping the bowl occasionally. Add the flour gradually, beating until blended. Knead on a floured pastry cloth until smooth and elastic. Place in a buttered bowl, turning to coat the surface. Let rise, covered, until doubled in bulk. Shape into 2 loaves in 2 buttered 5x9-inch loaf pans. Let rise, covered, until doubled in bulk. Bake at 400 degrees for 45 minutes. *Yield: 2 loaves.*

Connie Duey

French Bread I

1 envelope dry yeast
1 1/2 cups lukewarm water
2 tablespoons melted unsalted butter
4 cups all-purpose flour
1 cup cake flour
1 tablespoon sugar
2 teaspoons salt
Cornmeal
1 egg, beaten
1/2 teaspoon salt

Dissolve the yeast in the lukewarm water in a bowl. Stir in the butter. Mix the all-purpose flour, cake flour, sugar and 2 teaspoons salt in a bowl. Add to the yeast mixture 1 cup at a time, stirring until a stiff dough forms. Knead on a lightly floured surface for 10 minutes or until no longer sticky. Place in an oiled bowl, turning to coat the surface. Let rise, covered, in a warm place for 1 1/2 to 2 hours or until doubled in bulk.

Divide the dough into 2 portions. Roll each portion on a lightly floured surface to the desired length; tightly roll to form a loaf. Turn ends under. Place seam side down in a French bread pan sprinkled with cornmeal. Cut 3 to 4 diagonal slashes in the top of each loaf. Let rise, covered, for 1 to 1 1/2 hours or until doubled in bulk. Brush the tops with a mixture of the egg and 1/2 teaspoon salt. Bake at 400 degrees for 30 to 35 minutes or until brown. *Yield: 2 loaves.*

Pam Finkel

French Bread II

1 envelope dry yeast
2 1/4 cups lukewarm water
1/4 cup melted shortening
1 tablespoon salt
1 tablespoon sugar
7 to 7 1/2 cups sifted flour
1 egg
1 to 2 tablespoons water
Sesame seeds to taste

Dissolve the yeast in 1/4 cup of the lukewarm water in a bowl. Mix the yeast mixture, remaining 2 cups lukewarm water, shortening, salt and sugar in a bowl. Add the flour gradually, stirring until a stiff dough forms. Knead on a lightly floured surface for 5 to 8 minutes or until smooth and elastic. Place in a greased bowl, turning to coat the surface. Let rise for 1 1/2 hours or until doubled in bulk. Punch the dough down. Let rise for 30 minutes.

Divide the dough into 2 portions. Shape each portion into a long slender loaf; taper the ends. Arrange on a baking sheet. Cut 3 to 4 diagonal slashes in the top of each loaf. Let rise for 45 to 60 minutes. Brush with a mixture of the egg and 1 to 2 tablespoons water. Sprinkle with sesame seeds. Bake at 425 degrees for 15 minutes. Reduce the oven temperature to 350 degrees. Bake for 20 to 25 minutes or until brown. *Yield: 2 loaves.*

Nova Therrien

Julekage

½ cup dark raisins	1 cup milk	2 eggs
1 to 2 tablespoons (about) flour	¾ cup sugar	½ to 1 cup chopped walnuts
1 large cake yeast	½ cup margarine	
¼ cup lukewarm water	1 teaspoon salt	1 teaspoon cardamom
	1 cup flour	Flour

Plump the raisins in hot water to cover in a bowl. Drain and pat dry. Toss with 1 to 2 tablespoons flour. Soften the yeast in the lukewarm water in a bowl and mix well. Scald the milk in a saucepan. Combine the milk, sugar, margarine and salt in a bowl and mix well. Cool to lukewarm. Add 1 cup flour and mix well. Stir in the yeast mixture. Add the eggs 1 at a time, mixing well after each addition. Stir in the raisins, walnuts and cardamom. Add enough flour to make an easily handled dough and mix well.

Knead on a lightly floured surface until smooth and elastic. Place the dough in a greased bowl, turning to coat the surface. Let rise until doubled in bulk. Punch the dough down. Divide the dough into 2 portions. Shape each portion into a loaf in a greased loaf pan. Let rise until level with the top of the pan. Bake at 375 degrees for 35 to 40 minutes or until brown. *Yield: 2 loaves.*

Kathleen Hoppenrath

Oatmeal Bread

2 cups milk, scalded	½ cup lukewarm water	1 tablespoon melted butter
1 cup rolled oats	½ cup molasses	
1 envelope dry yeast	2 teaspoons salt	4½ cups flour

Pour the milk over the oats in a bowl. Let stand until lukewarm. Dissolve the yeast in the lukewarm water in a bowl. Stir the yeast mixture, molasses, salt and butter into the oats mixture. Add ½ of the flour, mixing until blended. Add the remaining flour and mix well. Let rise, covered, until light. Divide the dough into 2 portions. Shape each portion into a loaf in a greased 5x9-inch loaf pan. Let rise until doubled in bulk. Bake at 425 degrees for 15 minutes. Reduce the oven temperature to 350 degrees. Bake for 35 minutes longer. Remove to a wire rack to cool. *Yield: 2 loaves.*

Susan Van Dusen

Swedish Rye Bread

2 envelopes dry yeast
2 1/2 cups lukewarm water
1/2 cup molasses
1/2 cup packed brown sugar
1/2 cup corn syrup
2 tablespoons salt
10 cups all-purpose flour
2 cups rye flour

Dissolve the yeast in 1/2 cup of the lukewarm water in a bowl. Combine the remaining 2 cups lukewarm water, molasses, brown sugar, corn syrup and salt in a bowl and mix well. Stir in the yeast mixture. Add the all-purpose flour and rye flour and mix well. Knead on a lightly floured surface until smooth and elastic. Place the dough in a greased bowl, turning to coat the surface. Let rise until doubled in bulk. Punch the dough down. Divide the dough into 2 portions. Shape each portion into a loaf. Place on a baking sheet. Let rise until doubled in bulk. Bake at 300 degrees for 1 hour. *Yield: 2 loaves.*

Esther Wightman

White Bread

1 envelope dry yeast, or 1 cake yeast
1/4 cup lukewarm water
1/4 cup sugar
3 tablespoons shortening
2 teaspoons salt
1 3/4 cups milk, scalded
5 1/2 cups flour
Melted shortening or butter

Dissolve the yeast in the lukewarm water in a bowl. Combine the sugar, 3 tablespoons shortening and salt in a bowl. Add the milk, stirring until the shortening melts. Beat in 2 cups of the flour. Cool slightly if needed to a temperature not more than 100 degrees. Stir in the yeast mixture and 3 cups of the remaining flour. Sprinkle the remaining 1/2 cup flour on a hard surface. Knead the dough on the floured surface until smooth and elastic. The dough will develop a nonsticky satiny texture. Place the dough in a greased bowl, turning to coat the surface.

Let rise, covered, in a warm place until doubled in bulk. Punch the dough down. Let rise until almost doubled in bulk. Divide the dough into 2 portions. Let rest, covered, for 10 minutes. Shape each portion into a loaf in a greased loaf pan. Brush with melted shortening. Let rise until doubled in bulk. Bake at 375 degrees for 30 to 40 minutes or until brown. Invert onto wire racks to cool. *Yield: 2 loaves.*

Jessie Joy

French Croissants

1 envelope dry yeast
1 cup lukewarm water
3/4 cup evaporated milk
1/3 cup sugar
1/4 cup melted butter
1 1/2 teaspoons salt
1 egg, lightly beaten
1 cup butter, chilled
4 cups flour
1 egg, beaten
1 tablespoon water

Dissolve the yeast in 1 cup lukewarm water in a bowl. Stir in the evaporated milk, sugar, 1/4 cup melted butter, salt and 1 egg until blended. Cut 1 cup butter into the flour in a bowl until crumbly. Add the yeast mixture, stirring just until moistened. Chill, covered with plastic wrap, for 4 hours or up to 4 days. Knead on a lightly floured surface 6 to 8 times. Divide the dough into 4 portions. Roll 1 portion at a time into a 17-inch circle; keep the remaining dough in the refrigerator until needed. Cut each circle into 8 wedges. Roll up from the wide end. Shape into crescents on an ungreased baking sheet. Let rise, covered with a tea towel, for 1 hour. Brush the tops with a mixture of 1 egg and 1 tablespoon water. Bake at 325 degrees for 30 to 35 minutes. May be frozen before baking for future use. Do not substitute margarine for the butter in this recipe. *Yield: 32 croissants.*

Lornie Porter

Aunt Jessie's Old Southern Buttermilk Rolls

1 cake yeast
2 cups buttermilk
4 cups flour
1 tablespoon sugar
1/2 teaspoon baking soda
1/4 teaspoon baking powder
1 teaspoon salt
3 tablespoons lard
1 tablespoon sugar

Combine the yeast and buttermilk in a bowl, stirring until dissolved. Sift the flour, 1 tablespoon sugar, baking soda, baking powder and salt into a bowl and mix well. Beat the lard and 1 tablespoon sugar in a bowl until creamy. Add the buttermilk mixture and flour mixture and mix well. Roll 1/2 inch thick on a lightly floured surface. Cut with a biscuit cutter; fold over. Arrange on a greased baking sheet. Let rise for 1 hour. Bake at 375 degrees until light brown. *Yield: 24 rolls.*

Ethel Ross

Famous Rolls

1 1/2 envelopes dry yeast
1/4 cup (110-degree) water
1 cup milk, scalded
1/4 cup shortening
1/4 cup sugar
1 teaspoon salt
1 egg, beaten
3 1/2 cups sifted flour

Dissolve the yeast in the water in a bowl. Combine the milk, shortening, sugar and salt in a bowl and mix well. Cool to lukewarm. Stir in the yeast mixture and egg. Add the flour gradually, stirring until a soft dough forms. Place in a greased bowl, turning to coat the surface. Let rise, covered, in a warm place for 2 hours or until doubled in bulk. Shape into rolls as desired. Arrange in a greased baking pan. Let rise until doubled in bulk. Bake at 350 degrees for 15 to 20 minutes or until light brown. *Yield: 18 to 24 rolls.*

Jeannette Doud

Feather Bed Rolls

1 cake yeast
1/2 cup lukewarm water
2 1/2 cups milk
1/2 cup shortening
2 teaspoons sugar
5 cups flour
1 teaspoon salt

Dissolve the yeast in the lukewarm water in a bowl. Scald the milk in a saucepan. Stir in the shortening and sugar. Let stand until cool. Stir in the yeast mixture. Add a sifted mixture of the flour and salt gradually, beating until blended. Place the dough in a greased bowl, turning to coat the surface. Let rise until doubled in bulk. Beat the dough down. Fill muffin cups 1/3 full. Let rise until doubled in bulk. Bake at 350 degrees for 20 minutes. *Yield: 24 to 30 rolls.*

Agnes Michalke

Refrigerator Rolls

1 cake yeast	1 cup mashed potatoes	2 eggs
1/2 cup lukewarm water	2/3 cup shortening	6 to 8 cups sifted flour
1 cup milk	1/2 cup sugar	Melted butter
	1 teaspoon salt	

Dissolve the yeast in the lukewarm water in a bowl. Scald the milk in a saucepan. Cool to lukewarm. Add the yeast mixture to the milk and mix well. Beat the mashed potatoes, shortening, sugar, salt and eggs in a mixer bowl until creamy. Stir in the milk mixture. Add just enough of the flour to make a stiff dough and mix well. Knead on a lightly floured surface until smooth and elastic. Place in a greased bowl, turning to coat the surface. Let rise until doubled in bulk. Knead lightly. Brush with melted butter. Place in a bowl. Chill, tightly covered, in the refrigerator.

Shape the dough into rolls 1 hour prior to baking. Place on a baking sheet. Let rise, covered, until light. Bake at 400 degrees for 15 to 20 minutes or until brown. For variety, roll the dough 1/2 inch thick on a lightly floured surface. Sprinkle with shredded cheese; roll as for a jelly roll. Cut into 2-inch slices; place in muffin cups. Let rise until doubled in bulk. Bake at 400 degrees until brown. *Yield: 36 to 42 rolls.*

Pauline Solomon

Sticky Hot Cross Buns

1 envelope dry yeast	1 teaspoon salt	1/2 teaspoon mace
1/4 cup lukewarm water	3 1/2 to 4 cups sifted flour	Butter, softened
3/4 cup milk, scalded	1 cup coarsely chopped dates	1 egg white, lightly beaten
1/2 cup shortening	2 eggs, beaten	Confectioners' Sugar Icing
1/3 cup sugar	1/2 teaspoon cinnamon	Date slivers or jam

Dissolve the yeast in the lukewarm water in a bowl. Combine the milk, shortening, sugar and salt in a bowl, stirring until the shortening dissolves. Cool to lukewarm. Stir in the yeast mixture. Add the flour, dates, eggs, cinnamon and mace and mix well. Place in a greased bowl, turning to coat the surface. Brush the top with butter. Let rise, covered, until doubled in bulk. Knead on a lightly floured surface for 1 minute. Shape into eighteen 2-inch balls. Arrange the balls 1/2 inch apart in a greased baking pan. Brush with the egg white. Let rise, covered with a tea towel, until doubled in bulk. Bake at 375 degrees for 20 minutes or until brown. Remove to a wire rack to cool. Spread with Confectioners' Sugar Icing. Top with date slivers or jam in a crisscross pattern. *Yield: 18 to 24 buns.*

Confectioners' Sugar Icing

1 1/2 cups confectioners' sugar	2 to 2 1/2 tablespoons hot water	1/2 teaspoon vanilla extract

Combine the confectioners' sugar with the hot water in a bowl, stirring until of spreading consistency. Stir in the vanilla.

Mrs. George Clark

Pecan Twists

2 envelopes dry yeast	¼ cup sugar	Melted butter
¼ cup lukewarm water	2 eggs, beaten	½ cup packed brown sugar
4½ cups sifted flour	1 teaspoon salt	2 teaspoons cinnamon
1 cup lukewarm milk	1 teaspoon grated lemon peel	¾ cup chopped pecans
1 cup margarine, softened		

Dissolve the yeast in the lukewarm water in a bowl. Combine the yeast mixture, flour, milk, margarine, sugar, eggs, salt and lemon peel in a mixer bowl. Beat until smooth; dough will be very soft. Chill, covered with a damp tea towel, for 2 to 10 hours. Divide the dough into 2 portions. Roll each portion into a 12-inch square on a lightly floured surface. Brush with melted butter.

Combine the brown sugar and cinnamon in a bowl and mix well. Sprinkle each dough square with 2 tablespoons of the cinnamon mixture; sprinkle with some of the pecans. Fold ⅓ of the square over the center third of each square. Sprinkle with the remaining cinnamon mixture and the remaining pecans. Fold each remaining third over the two layers. Cut crosswise into 1-inch strips. Twist the ends in opposite directions; seal the ends. Arrange 1½ inches apart on a greased baking sheet. Let rise for 1 hour. Bake at 400 degrees for 20 minutes. Frost if desired. *Yield: 2 dozen twists.*

Mary M. Smith

Cinnamon Twists

1 cup sour cream
3 tablespoons sugar
1 tablespoon shortening
1 tablespoon salt
1/8 teaspoon baking soda
1 large egg

1 cake yeast, or
1 envelope dry yeast
3 cups sifted flour
2 tablespoons butter or
margarine, softened

1 teaspoon cinnamon
1/2 cup packed
brown sugar
3/4 cup confectioners'
sugar
1 tablespoon milk

Bring the sour cream to a boil in a saucepan. Remove from heat. Stir in the sugar, shortening, salt and baking soda. Cool to lukewarm. Add the egg and yeast, stirring until the yeast dissolves. Stir in the flour. Knead on a lightly floured surface for 15 to 20 seconds or until a soft ball forms. Let rest, covered with a damp tea towel, for 5 minutes. Roll into a 6x24-inch rectangle 1/4 inch thick. Spread with the butter. Sprinkle 1/2 of the rectangle with a mixture of the cinnamon and brown sugar.

Fold the buttered half of the rectangle over the sugared half, forming a 3x24-inch rectangle; seal the ends. Cut the rectangle into twenty-four 1-inch strips. Twist the ends of each strip in opposite directions. Arrange on a greased baking sheet, pressing both ends of each twist firmly onto the baking sheet. Let rise, covered, in a warm place for 1 1/4 hours or until light.

Bake at 375 degrees for 12 to 15 minutes or until brown. Drizzle a mixture of the confectioners' sugar and milk over the warm twists. For sour cream, add 1 tablespoon vinegar to 1 cup cream or 1 cup diluted evaporated milk. Let stand for 5 minutes. *Yield: 24 twists.*

June Brown

Ukrainian Kolache

1 envelope dry yeast	1 tablespoon shortening	4 cups flour
1/2 cup lukewarm water	1 tablespoon sugar	2 eggs
1 cup milk, scalded	1 1/2 teaspoons salt	2 tablespoons water

Dissolve the yeast in 1/2 cup lukewarm water in a bowl. Combine the milk, shortening, sugar and salt in a bowl, stirring until the shortening melts. Cool to lukewarm. Add 1 1/2 cups of the flour, beating until blended. Add the yeast mixture and 1 of the eggs and mix well. Add 2 cups of the remaining flour, beating until blended. Sprinkle the remaining 1/2 cup flour on a hard surface. Knead the dough on the floured surface until smooth and elastic. Place in a greased bowl, turning to coat the surface.

Let rise, covered, until doubled in bulk. Divide the dough into 8 portions. Roll each portion into a 2-inch-long rope. Twist 2 of the ropes together. Repeat the process with the remaining dough ropes. Braid 3 of the twists into a circle on a greased baking sheet. Encircle with the remaining twist. Let rise, covered, until doubled in bulk. Brush with a mixture of the remaining egg and 2 tablespoons water. Bake at 375 degrees for 25 minutes. *Yield: 16 servings.*

Stella King

Cinnamon Sticks

1/2 cup butter, softened	2 cups flour	Cinnamon and sugar
1/2 cup shortening	1/2 teaspoon vanilla	to taste
5 tablespoons sugar	extract	

Beat the butter, shortening and sugar in a mixer bowl until creamy, scraping the bowl occasionally. Add the flour and vanilla and mix well. Shape the dough into small sticks. Roll in cinnamon and sugar. Arrange on a baking sheet. Bake at 375 degrees for 5 minutes or until brown. Roll in cinnamon and sugar. *Yield: 40 to 48 servings.*

Esther Wightman

For-Sure Popovers

1 cup flour	1/2 teaspoon salt	1 cup milk
	2 eggs	

Sift the flour and salt together. Combine the eggs, milk and flour mixture in a bowl, stirring just until moistened. Disregard the lumps. Fill 6 greased custard cups 3/4 full. Set the custard cups in muffin cups. Place in a cold oven. Bake at 450 degrees for 30 minutes; do not open the oven door. Remove from the oven. Make slits in each of the popovers. Bake for 10 minutes longer. May reheat on a baking sheet at 350 degrees for 10 minutes.
Yield: 6 popovers.

Mrs. George Clark

Doughnuts

3 3/4 cups flour	1/4 teaspoon nutmeg	2 eggs, beaten
4 teaspoons baking powder	1/4 teaspoon cinnamon	1 cup milk
	1 cup sugar	Vegetable oil, shortening
1/2 teaspoon salt	2 tablespoons shortening	or lard for deep-frying

Combine the flour, baking powder, salt, nutmeg and cinnamon in a bowl and mix well. Beat the sugar and 2 tablespoons shortening in a mixer bowl until light and fluffy, scraping the bowl occasionally. Stir in the eggs. Add 1 cup of the dry ingredients alternately with 1/4 cup of the milk until all of the ingredients are used, beating well after each addition. Chill, covered, for several hours. Roll the dough on a lightly floured surface; cut with a doughnut cutter. Add enough oil to a deep fryer to measure 4 inches. Heat the oil to 390 degrees on a cooking thermometer. Deep-fry the doughnuts in the hot oil for 3 minutes or until light brown on both sides, turning once; drain. *Yield: 18 to 20 doughnuts.*

Sara Chambers

Rosettes

½ cup milk
1 egg, lightly beaten
1 teaspoon sugar
½ teaspoon salt
½ teaspoon vegetable oil
½ cup sifted flour
Vegetable oil for frying

Combine the milk, egg, sugar, salt and ½ teaspoon oil in a bowl and mix well. Sift the flour into the milk mixture, beating constantly until smooth. Let stand for 1 hour or until the mixture is free of bubbles. The batter will be thin. Fry in hot oil in a skillet with a rosette iron using manufacturer's directions. *Yield: variable.*

Esther Wightman

Yorkshire Pudding

6 tablespoons flour
1 teaspoon salt
2 eggs
⅔ cup milk
⅓ cup water
Pan drippings

Combine the flour and salt in a bowl and mix well. Stir in the eggs, milk and water. Beat with a spoon until of the consistency of thick cream. Let stand at room temperature for several hours, stirring occasionally. Every hour it stands enhances its flavor. Pour hot pan drippings from a beef roast into a 10x10-inch baking pan. May add additional shortening if desired. Heat the pan drippings in a 425-degree oven until smoking. Pour in the batter. Bake for 30 minutes or until brown and crisp around the edges. Serve immediately with beef roast and gravy. *Yield: 6 to 8 servings.*

Vera Beall

Sweet Endings

Desserts

Apple Crumb Pie Dessert

7 cups sliced peeled apples
1/3 cup orange juice or lemon juice
3/4 cup flour
1/2 cup sugar

1/2 cup packed brown sugar
2 teaspoons grated orange or lemon peel
1/2 teaspoon nutmeg
1/2 teaspoon (or more) cinnamon

1/4 teaspoon salt
1/3 cup butter or margarine
1 pint ice cream

Arrange the apples in a deep round baking dish; drizzle with the orange juice. Combine the flour, sugar, brown sugar, orange peel, nutmeg, cinnamon and salt in a bowl and mix well. Cut in the butter until crumbly. Sprinkle over the apples. Bake at 350 degrees for 1 hour. Serve warm with the ice cream. *Yield: 8 servings.*

Helga R. Doud

Apple Crisp

6 tart apples, peeled, sliced
1/2 cup sugar
1/4 cup water

2 teaspoons lemon juice
1/2 teaspoon cinnamon
3/4 cup flour

1/2 cup sugar
1/4 teaspoon salt
6 tablespoons butter or margarine

Combine the apples, 1/2 cup sugar, water, lemon juice and cinnamon in a bowl, tossing to mix. Spoon into an 8x8-inch baking pan. Combine the flour, 1/2 cup sugar and salt in a bowl and mix well. Cut in the butter until crumbly. Pat the mixture over the apples. Bake at 375 degrees for 40 to 50 minutes or until the apples are tender and the topping is brown. May substitute 2 to 3 teaspoons red hot cinnamon candies for the cinnamon.
Yield: 6 to 8 servings.

Mabel Breuckman

Cherries and Chocolate

1 package frozen Michigan cherries, thawed, pitted
1 package frozen dark sweet cherries, thawed, pitted
2 dark bittersweet Dove candy bars, crumbled
2 cups whipping cream, whipped
Shaved chocolate or baking cocoa

Combine the cherries in a bowl and toss gently. Spoon into crystal dessert bowls or wine goblets. Sprinkle with the candy bars. Chill in the refrigerator. Top with whipped cream and shaved chocolate just before serving. *Yield: 6 to 8 servings.*

Candi Dunnigan

Pineapple Cheesecake

20 graham crackers, crushed
Melted butter
1 (6-ounce) package lemon gelatin
1 cup boiling water
8 ounces cream cheese, softened
$1/2$ cup sugar
1 cup crushed drained pineapple
3 tablespoons lemon juice
1 (12-ounce) can evaporated milk, chilled

Combine the graham cracker crumbs and butter in a bowl, stirring until crumbly. Dissolve the gelatin in the boiling water in a mixer bowl and mix well. Chill until partially set. Beat until light and fluffy. Beat the cream cheese and sugar in a mixer bowl until creamy. Add the cream cheese mixture, pineapple and lemon juice to the gelatin mixture and mix well. Beat the evaporated milk in a bowl until soft peaks form. Stir into the gelatin mixture. Sprinkle $1/2$ of the crumb mixture in a 9x13-inch dish. Spread with the cream cheese mixture. Sprinkle with the remaining crumb mixture. Chill until set. May spoon the cream cheese mixture into 3 graham cracker pie shells. *Yield: 15 servings.*

Caroline LaPine

Cream Cheese Dessert

24 graham crackers, crushed
1/2 cup melted butter
1/4 cup sugar

12 ounces cream cheese, softened
1 cup confectioners' sugar

3 envelopes whipped topping mix, prepared
1 (21-ounce) can pie filling

Combine the graham cracker crumbs, butter and sugar in a bowl and mix well. Spread in a 9x13-inch baking pan. Bake at 350 degrees for 10 minutes. Let stand until cool. Beat the cream cheese and confectioners' sugar in a mixer bowl until smooth, scraping the bowl occasionally. Add the whipped topping gradually, mixing until blended. Spread over the baked layer. Chill for 8 to 10 hours. Spread with the pie filling. *Yield: 15 servings.*

Sally Dufina

Cheesecake

24 graham crackers, crushed
1/2 cup melted butter or margarine

3 tablespoons sugar
4 cups cottage cheese
3/4 cup sugar
3/4 cup half-and-half or milk

2 tablespoons flour
1 teaspoon vanilla extract
4 eggs, beaten
1/8 teaspoon salt

Combine the graham cracker crumbs, butter and 3 tablespoons sugar in a bowl and mix well. Pat 1/2 of the mixture into a 9x13-inch baking pan; press firmly. Combine the cottage cheese, 3/4 cup sugar, half-and-half, flour, vanilla, eggs and salt in a bowl and mix well. Spread over the prepared layer. Top with the remaining crumb mixture. Bake at 350 degrees for 1 hour. Serve warm or cold. *Yield: 15 servings.*

Ruby Bloswick

Cream Puffs

1 cup water	¼ teaspoon salt	Vanilla Filling
½ cup margarine	1 cup flour	Chocolate Glaze
	4 eggs	

Combine the water, margarine and salt in a saucepan. Bring to a boil. Boil until the margarine melts. Add the flour all at once, stirring with a wooden spoon until the mixture forms a ball. Remove from heat. Add the eggs 1 at a time, beating well after each addition. Cool slightly. Spoon 10 mounds onto a lightly greased and floured baking sheet. Bake at 400 degrees for 40 minutes. Turn off oven. Let stand in oven with the door closed for 15 minutes. Remove to a wire rack to cool. Fill each cream puff with the Vanilla Filling; drizzle with the Chocolate Glaze. *Yield: 10 servings.*

Vanilla Filling

1 (4-ounce) package vanilla instant pudding mix	1¼ cups milk 1 cup whipping cream	1 teaspoon almond extract

Prepare the pudding mix using package directions and substituting 1¼ cups milk for the milk. Beat the whipping cream and almond flavoring in a mixer bowl until soft peaks form. Fold into the pudding.

Chocolate Glaze

½ cup semisweet chocolate chips	1 tablespoon margarine 1½ teaspoons milk	1½ teaspoons light corn syrup

Combine the chocolate chips, margarine, milk and corn syrup in a double boiler. Cook until blended, stirring frequently.

Joanne Zwolinski

So-Easy Cream Puffs

1 cup water
½ cup butter
1 cup flour
4 eggs
1 teaspoon vanilla extract
Ice cream

Bring the water and butter to a rolling boil in a saucepan. Remove from heat. Stir in the flour. Let stand until cool. Add the eggs 1 at a time, mixing well after each addition. Stir in the vanilla. Drop by heaping tablespoonfuls onto a baking sheet. Bake at 400 degrees for 15 minutes. Reduce the oven temperature to 350 degrees. Bake for 35 minutes longer. Remove to a wire rack to cool. Slice and fill with your favorite ice cream.
Yield: 8 to 10 servings.

Sandy King

Slip Custard

3 cups milk
⅔ cup sugar
4 eggs
½ teaspoon nutmeg
⅛ teaspoon cinnamon

Combine the milk, sugar, eggs, nutmeg and cinnamon in a bowl, whisking until blended. Pour into a baking dish. Place the baking dish in a baking pan. Fill the baking pan with enough cold water to reach halfway up the sides of the baking dish. Bake at 450 degrees for 10 minutes. Reduce the oven temperature to 310 degrees. Bake for 45 minutes longer or until set. *Yield: 4 to 6 servings.*

Margie Murphy

Six Threes Ice Cream

3 bananas, mashed
Juice of 3 oranges
Juice of 3 lemons
3 cups sugar
3 cups milk
3 cups cream

Mix the bananas, orange juice and lemon juice in a bowl; set aside. Combine the sugar, milk and cream in a bowl and mix well. Pour into an ice cream freezer container. Freeze until of a slushy consistency. Add the banana mixture and mix well. Freeze until set.
Yield: 8 to 10 servings.

Selma Dufina

Fruit and Nut Bread Pudding

16 slices dry bread, torn into 1-inch pieces
2 cups sugar
4 eggs
3 cups milk
2 tablespoons vanilla extract
2 teaspoons cinnamon
1/2 teaspoon salt
1 (21-ounce) can apple pie filling
2 cups chopped pecans
1 cup golden raisins
3/4 cup melted butter or margarine

Combine the bread and sugar in a bowl. Beat the eggs, milk, vanilla, cinnamon and salt in a mixer bowl until blended. Pour over the bread mixture, stirring to mix. Chill, covered, for 2 hours. Stir in the pie filling, pecans, raisins and butter. Spoon into a greased 9x13-inch baking pan. Bake at 350 degrees for 45 to 50 minutes or until brown and bubbly.
Yield: 15 servings.

Gracie Koerbel

English Plum Pudding

1 cup flour
1 teaspoon baking soda
1 teaspoon salt
1 teaspoon cinnamon
3/4 teaspoon mace
1/4 teaspoon nutmeg
2 cups currants

1 1/2 cups raisins
1 1/2 cups bread crumbs
3/4 cup chopped citron
1/2 cup chopped walnuts
1/4 cup chopped candied orange peel
1/4 cup chopped candied lemon peel

2 cups ground suet
1 cup packed brown sugar
1/3 cup currant jelly
1/4 cup fruit juice
3 eggs
Hard Sauce

Combine the flour, baking soda, salt, cinnamon, mace and nutmeg in a bowl and mix well. Stir in the currants, raisins, bread crumbs, citron, walnuts, orange peel and lemon peel. Combine the suet, brown sugar, jelly, fruit juice and eggs in a bowl and mix well. Add to the flour mixture and mix well. Spoon into a greased plum pudding mold. Place the mold in a Dutch oven. Add enough water to cover the bottom of the Dutch oven. Steam, covered, for 4 hours or until a wooden pick inserted in the center comes out clean. Serve with the Hard Sauce. May soak the plum pudding in brandy or rum and flame just before serving.
Yield: 6 to 8 servings.

Hard Sauce

5 tablespoons butter, softened
1 cup confectioners' sugar
1 teaspoon vanilla extract
1/8 teaspoon salt

Beat the butter in a mixer bowl until creamy. Add the confectioners' sugar gradually, beating until blended. Beat in the vanilla and salt until smooth. Chill, covered, until serving time. May substitute 1 tablespoon sherry, brandy, rum, whiskey, lemon juice or coffee for the vanilla.

Trish Martin

Lemon Sponge Pudding

1 cup sugar	1/4 cup flour	1 1/2 cups milk
2 tablespoons butter, softened	Grated peel and juice of 1 lemon	3 egg yolks, beaten
	Salt to taste	3 egg whites, beaten

Beat the sugar and butter in a mixer bowl until creamy. Add the flour, lemon peel, lemon juice and salt and mix well. Stir in a mixture of the milk and egg yolks. Fold in the egg whites. Spoon into a soufflé dish. Place in a baking pan with hot water to reach halfway up the side of the soufflé dish. Bake at 350 degrees for 45 minutes. Serve with hard sauce. Yield: 6 servings.

Nan Rudolph

Voletta Cherry Pudding

1 cup sugar	2 cups drained sour cherries	1/2 cup packed brown sugar
1 1/2 cups flour	1 teaspoon vanilla extract	1/2 cup chopped nuts
1 teaspoon baking soda	1 tablespoon butter, melted	
1/2 teaspoon salt		
1 egg, beaten		

Combine the sugar, flour, baking soda and salt in a bowl and mix well. Stir in the egg, sour cherries and vanilla in the order given. Spoon the cherry mixture into a baking pan. Drizzle with the butter and sprinkle with the brown sugar and nuts. Bake at 325 degrees for 1 hour. Yield: 4 to 6 servings.

Mrs. John W. Claxton

Mackinac Plum Crunch

3 cups pitted blue plums, cut into quarters
3 tablespoons brown sugar
5 tablespoons sugar
1/4 teaspoon nutmeg
1 cup flour
1 cup sugar
1 teaspoon baking powder
1/4 teaspoon salt
1 egg, beaten
1/2 cup melted butter

Arrange the plums in a 7x10-inch baking pan. Combine the brown sugar, 5 tablespoons sugar and nutmeg in a bowl and mix well. Sprinkle over the plums. Combine the flour, 1 cup sugar, baking powder, salt and egg in a bowl, mixing with a pastry cutter until crumbly. Sprinkle over the prepared layers; drizzle with the butter. Bake at 375 degrees for 45 minutes. Serve warm. *Yield: 6 to 8 servings.*

Mabel Breuckman

Prune Whip

8 ounces prunes
2/3 cup sugar
Grated lemon peel to taste
1 cup port
1 cup whipping cream
3 tablespoons confectioners' sugar

Soak the prunes in water to cover in a bowl overnight; drain. Combine the prunes, sugar, lemon peel and enough water to cover in a saucepan. Bring to a boil; reduce heat. Cook until the prunes are tender; drain. Stir in the port. Cook for 10 minutes longer, stirring occasionally. Remove from heat. Press the prunes through a sieve into a bowl. May add additional wine if prunes are too dry. Add additional sugar if desired. Beat the whipping cream in a mixer bowl until soft peaks form. Fold 1/2 of the whipped cream into the prune mixture. Spoon into serving bowls. Mix the confectioners' sugar with the remaining whipped cream. Top each serving with the sweetened whipped cream. *Yield: 6 servings.*

Susan VanDusen

Chocolate Fondue

1 cup semisweet
chocolate chips

½ cup sugar
½ cup milk

½ cup creamy
peanut butter

Combine the chocolate chips, sugar and milk in a double boiler. Cook until blended, stirring constantly. Add the peanut butter. Cook until blended, stirring constantly. Spoon into a fondue pot. Serve with fresh fruit and/or pound cake. *Yield: 16 servings.*

Nancy Compton

Fudge Sauce

½ cup butter
1 (1-pound) package
confectioners' sugar

1 (12-ounce) can
evaporated milk
8 ounces chocolate,
coarsely chopped

⅛ teaspoon salt
1 teaspoon vanilla extract

Combine the butter, confectioners' sugar, evaporated milk, chocolate, and salt in a double boiler. Cook for 30 minutes, stirring frequently. Let stand until cool. Stir in the vanilla. May substitute 1¼ cups cream for the evaporated milk. *Yield: 1½ quarts.*

Grand Hotel

Divinity

3 cups sugar
¾ cup water

¾ cup light corn syrup
2 egg whites, stiffly beaten

1 cup broken nuts
1 teaspoon vanilla extract

Combine the sugar, water and corn syrup in a saucepan. Cook until the sugar dissolves, stirring constantly. Cook to 252 degrees on a candy thermometer, hard-ball stage; do not stir. Remove from heat. Add the hot syrup in a fine stream to the egg whites, beating constantly. Beat until the mixture holds its shape and loses its gloss. Add the nuts and vanilla and mix well. Drop by teaspoonfuls onto waxed paper. Let stand until firm. *Yield: 2 pounds.*

Jeannette Doud

Easy No-Bake Cookies

2 cups sugar
1/2 cup butter or margarine
1/2 cup milk
3 cups quick-cooking oats
1 cup peanut butter
6 tablespoons baking cocoa
1 teaspoon vanilla extract

Bring the sugar, butter and milk to a boil in a saucepan. Boil for 1 minute. Remove from heat. Stir in the oats, peanut butter, baking cocoa and vanilla. Drop by teaspoonfuls onto waxed paper. Let stand until firm. *Yield: 3 dozen.*

Stephanie and Andrew McGreevy
Debora Carley

Million-Dollar Fudge

12 ounces German's sweet chocolate, coarsely chopped
2 cups chopped nuts
2 cups semisweet chocolate chips
1 pint marshmallow creme
4 1/2 cups sugar
1 (12-ounce) can evaporated milk
2 tablespoons butter
1/8 teaspoon salt

Combine the German's sweet chocolate, nuts, chocolate chips and marshmallow creme in a bowl. Bring the sugar, evaporated milk, butter and salt to a boil in a saucepan. Boil for 6 minutes. Pour over the chocolate mixture, beating until the chocolate melts. Spread in a greased shallow dish. Let stand until set. Cut into squares. Store in an airtight container. *Yield: 4 pounds.*

Barbara Sosnowski

Superior Fudge

2 packages chocolate chips
1/2 cup chopped walnuts
1/4 cup butter, cut into pieces
1/2 teaspoon salt
1/2 teaspoon vanilla extract
1/4 teaspoon peppermint extract
2 cups sugar
1 cup evaporated milk
12 large marshmallows, cut into halves

Combine the chocolate chips, walnuts, butter, salt and flavorings in a bowl. Combine the sugar, evaporated milk and marshmallows in a saucepan. Bring to a rolling boil; reduce heat. Cook for 5 minutes, stirring constantly with a wooden spoon. Pour over the chocolate chip mixture and mix well. Spread in a buttered 8x8-inch dish. Let stand until set. *Yield: 1 1/2 pounds.*

Eileen Hunt

Won't-Fail Fudge

1 (5-ounce) can evaporated milk
16 large marshmallows
1 1/3 cups sugar
1/4 cup butter
1/4 teaspoon salt
1 1/2 cups semisweet chocolate chips
1 cup coarsely chopped walnuts or pecans
1 teaspoon vanilla extract

Bring the evaporated milk, marshmallows, sugar, butter and salt to a boil in a saucepan. Boil for 5 minutes, stirring constantly. Remove from heat. Add the chocolate chips, stirring until melted. Stir in the walnuts and vanilla. Spread in a buttered 8x8-inch dish. Let stand until set. *Yield: 2 pounds.*

Mrs. Earl Chapin

Peanut Butter Bars

4 cups peanut butter
2/3 cup melted butter
4 cups confectioners' sugar
1 cup nonfat dry milk powder
2 cups chocolate chips, melted

Heat the peanut butter and butter in a saucepan until blended, stirring constantly. Remove from heat. Stir in a sifted mixture of the confectioners' sugar and milk powder. Spread in a 9x13-inch dish. Drizzle with the melted chocolate chips. Chill until set. Cut into bars. Store in the refrigerator. *Yield: 36 bars.*

Stephanie and Andrew McGreevy

English Toffee

1 cup sugar
1 cup butter
3 tablespoons water
1 teaspoon vanilla extract
3 chocolate candy bars
3/4 cup chopped pecans

Combine the sugar, butter and water in a saucepan. Cook for 10 minutes or until brown in color, stirring constantly. Stir in the vanilla. Pour into a buttered dish. Arrange the candy bars on top of the hot mixture; sprinkle with the pecans. Let stand until cool. Break into pieces. *Yield: 2 pounds.*

Mrs. E. J. Harmon

Apple Cake

4 cups chopped unpeeled apples
2 cups sugar
1 1/2 teaspoons cinnamon
1 teaspoon salt
3 cups flour
1 teaspoon baking soda
2 eggs
1 1/4 cups vegetable oil
1 1/2 teaspoons vanilla extract
1 cup chopped nuts

Combine the apples, sugar, cinnamon, salt, flour, baking soda, eggs, oil, vanilla and nuts in the order listed in a bowl and mix well. Spoon into an ungreased 9x13-inch cake pan. Bake at 350 degrees for 1 hour. *Yield: 15 servings.*

Louann Mosley

Banana Cake

2 1/2 cups flour
1 1/2 cups sugar
1 1/2 teaspoons baking powder
1 teaspoon baking soda
1 teaspoon salt
1 cup mashed bananas
1/2 cup shortening
2/3 cup buttermilk or sour milk
2 eggs
1 teaspoon vanilla extract

Combine the flour, sugar, baking powder, baking soda and salt in a mixer bowl and mix well. Add the bananas and shortening. Beat at low speed until blended. Add the buttermilk, eggs and vanilla. Beat at medium speed for 2 minutes, scraping the bowl occasionally. Spoon into 2 greased and floured 9-inch cake pans. Bake at 350 degrees for 30 minutes. Cool in the pans for 5 to 10 minutes. Remove to a wire rack to cool completely. Spread your favorite frosting between the layers and over the top and side of the cake. *Yield: 12 servings.*

Debora Carley

Black Walnut Banana Cake

1 1/2 cups sugar
2/3 cup butter, softened
2 egg yolks
1/4 cup sour milk or buttermilk
1 teaspoon baking soda
1 1/2 cups flour
1/4 cup chopped black walnuts
1 cup mashed bananas
1 teaspoon (scant) salt
1 teaspoon vanilla extract
1/2 teaspoon baking powder
2 egg whites, beaten

Beat the sugar, butter and egg yolks in a mixer bowl until creamy, scraping the bowl occasionally. Beat in a mixture of the sour milk and baking soda. Combine the flour and walnuts in a bowl and mix well. Stir the flour mixture, bananas, salt, vanilla and baking powder into the creamed mixture. Fold in the egg whites. Spoon into a 9x9-inch cake pan or tube pan. Bake at 350 degrees for 45 to 50 minutes or until the cake tests done. Cool in the pan on a wire rack. Spread with your favorite butter frosting flavored with 1/2 teaspoon or more rum or brandy flavoring. *Yield: 12 servings.*

Marie Newell

Banana Sheet Cake

1 cup butter or margarine
½ cup water
2 cups sugar
1 cup mashed bananas
¼ cup milk
2 eggs
1 teaspoon baking soda
2 cups flour
Banana Frosting

Combine the butter and water in a saucepan. Bring to a boil. Remove from heat. Stir in the sugar, bananas, milk, eggs and baking soda. Add the flour and mix well. Spoon into an ungreased 10x15-inch cake pan. Bake at 350 degrees for 20 to 25 minutes or until the cake tests done. Spread the Banana Frosting over the hot cake. *Yield: 15 servings.*

Banana Frosting

1 (1-pound) package confectioners' sugar
⅓ cup mashed banana
¼ cup butter, softened
1 teaspoon vanilla extract

Combine the confectioners' sugar, banana, butter and vanilla in a mixer bowl. Beat until of spreading consistency, scraping the bowl occasionally.

Gracie Koerbel

Blueberry Cake

3 cups flour	⅓ teaspoon salt	2 eggs
1½ cups sugar	½ cup shortening	1½ cups blueberries
1 tablespoon baking powder	1 cup plus 2 tablespoons milk	Hard Sauce for Blueberry Cake

Sift the flour, sugar, baking powder and salt into a bowl and mix well. Beat the shortening in a mixer bowl until creamy. Add the flour mixture and milk. Beat for 2 minutes, scraping the bowl occasionally. Add the eggs. Beat for 1 minute. Stir in the blueberries. Spoon into a greased 5x9-inch cake pan. Bake at 350 degrees for 50 minutes or until the cake tests done. Cool slightly. Slice and serve with Hard Sauce for Blueberry Cake. *Yield: 12 servings.*

Hard Sauce for Blueberry Cake

| 1 cup butter, softened | 2 cups sifted confectioners' sugar | 1 teaspoon vanilla or rum extract |
| ⅛ teaspoon salt | | |

Beat the butter in a mixer bowl at high speed until creamy. Add the salt and confectioners' sugar gradually, beating well after each addition. Beat until of a sauce consistency, scraping the bowl occasionally. Stir in the vanilla. Chill, covered, for 1 hour. May substitute 1 tablespoon cooking sherry for the vanilla.

Hope Goodwin

Carrot Cake

1½ cups flour	½ teaspoon baking soda	½ cup shortening
1½ teaspoons cinnamon	½ teaspoon ground cloves	2 eggs
½ teaspoon baking powder	⅔ cup raisins	1 cup mashed cooked carrots
½ teaspoon salt	½ cup chopped nuts	3 tablespoons sour milk
	1 cup sugar	

Sift the flour, cinnamon, baking powder, salt, baking soda and cloves into a bowl and mix well. Stir in the raisins and nuts. Beat the sugar and shortening in a mixer bowl until creamy. Add the eggs 1 at a time, beating well after each addition. Stir in the carrots. Add the flour mixture and mix well. Stir in the sour milk. Spoon into a greased and floured 5x9-inch cake pan. Bake at 350 degrees for 50 to 60 minutes or until the cake tests done. May substitute baby food carrots for the mashed cooked carrots. *Yield: 12 servings.*

Mary Thompson

Chocolate Chip Date Cake

1 cup chopped dates	½ cup shortening	½ teaspoon salt
1 teaspoon baking soda	1 teaspoon vanilla extract	½ cup sugar
1½ cups boiling water	1½ cups plus 3 tablespoons flour	½ cup chocolate chips
1 cup sugar	¾ teaspoon baking soda	½ cup chopped nuts

Combine the dates and 1 teaspoon baking soda in a bowl and mix well. Pour the boiling water over the date mixture. Let stand at room temperature until cool. Beat 1 cup sugar, shortening and vanilla in a mixer bowl until creamy, scraping the bowl occasionally. Stir in the date mixture. Add the flour, ¾ teaspoon baking soda and salt and mix well. Spoon into a greased 9-inch cake pan. Sprinkle with ½ cup sugar, chocolate chips and nuts. Bake at 350 degrees for 40 minutes. Reduce the oven temperature to 300 degrees. Bake for 15 minutes longer. *Yield: 12 servings.*

Caroline LaPine

Company Cake

1 cup flour
1 teaspoon baking powder
1/4 teaspoon salt
1/2 cup shortening

1/2 cup sugar
4 egg yolks, beaten
1 teaspoon vanilla extract
5 tablespoons milk

4 egg whites
1 cup sugar
Chopped walnuts
Custard Filling

Sift the flour, baking powder and salt into a bowl and mix well. Beat the shortening and 1/2 cup sugar in a mixer bowl until creamy. Add the egg yolks and vanilla and mix well. Add the flour mixture alternately with the milk, beating well after each addition. Spoon into 2 greased and floured 8-inch cake pans. Beat the egg whites in a mixer bowl until foamy. Add 1 cup sugar gradually, beating constantly until stiff peaks form. Spread the meringue over the prepared layers; sprinkle with walnuts. Bake at 325 degrees for 40 minutes. Remove to a wire rack to cool. Arrange 1 of the cake layers on a cake plate. Spread with the Custard Filling. Top with the remaining cake layer. Spread whipped cream over the top if desired. *Yield: 12 servings.*

Custard Filling

2 tablespoons sugar
1 tablespoon cornstarch

1/8 teaspoon salt
1 cup milk
1 egg yolk

1/2 teaspoon vanilla extract

Combine the sugar, cornstarch and salt in a saucepan and mix well. Stir in the milk and egg yolk. Cook until thickened, stirring constantly. Remove from heat. Stir in the vanilla.

Marjorie Lang

Coronation Cake

1 1/2 cups flour
1 teaspoon baking powder
1/2 teaspoon salt
1 cup sugar

1/4 cup butter or
margarine, softened
1 egg
1 cup chopped dates

1 cup boiling water
1 teaspoon baking soda
1/2 cup chopped nuts
Coconut Icing

Sift the flour, baking powder and salt into a bowl. Cream the sugar, butter and egg in a mixer bowl. Add the flour mixture and mix well. Spoon into a saucepan. Bring to a boil, stirring constantly. Boil until thickened and pale in color, stirring constantly. Stir in the dates, boiling water and baking soda. Add the nuts and mix well. Spoon into a greased and floured 8x8- or 9x9-inch cake pan. Bake at 350 degrees for 32 minutes. Spoon the Coconut Icing over the warm cake. Bake for 10 minutes longer or until bubbly. *Yield: 8 to 12 servings.*

Coconut Icing

5 tablespoons sugar

3 tablespoons butter
2 tablespoons cream

1/2 cup shredded coconut

Combine the sugar, butter and cream in a saucepan. Bring to a boil, stirring constantly. Stir in the coconut.

Mrs. E. J. Harmon

Cream-Coated Devil's Food Cake

1 teaspoon baking soda
1/2 cup sour milk
1 tablespoon (heaping)
baking cocoa

1/2 cup hot water
2 cups packed
brown sugar
1/2 cup butter, softened
2 eggs

1/2 teaspoon salt
2 cups flour
1 teaspoon vanilla extract
Sweetened whipped cream

Dissolve the baking soda in the sour milk. Dissolve the baking cocoa in the hot water. Beat the brown sugar, butter, eggs and salt in a mixer bowl until creamy. Add the flour alternately with the milk mixture and cocoa mixture, beating constantly. Stir in the vanilla. Spoon into two 8-inch cake pans. Bake at 350 degrees for 25 to 30 minutes. Cool. Spread the whipped cream between the layers and over the top and side of the cake. *Yield: 12 servings.*

Florence Vance

Chocolate Pastry Cakes

8 ounces German's sweet chocolate
1/2 cup sugar
1/2 cup water
1 teaspoon cinnamon
2 teaspoons vanilla extract
1 (9-ounce) package pie crust mix
2 cups whipping cream
Chocolate curls

Combine the chocolate, sugar, water and cinnamon in a saucepan. Cook over low heat until smooth, stirring frequently. Remove from heat. Stir in the vanilla. Cool to room temperature. Mix 3/4 cup of the cooled chocolate mixture with the pie crust mix in a bowl. Divide the dough into 4 equal portions. Press each portion over the bottom and to within 1/2 inch of the edge of an inverted 8-inch round or square cake pan. Bake at 450 degrees until firm. Let stand until cool. Beat the whipping cream in a mixer bowl until soft peaks form. Fold in the remaining chocolate mixture. Spread between the pastries and over the tops. Sprinkle with chocolate curls. Chill for 8 hours or longer. *Yield: 12 servings.*

Pat Squires

Large Chocolate Sour Cream Sheet Cake

3 cups margarine
3 cups water
3/4 cup baking cocoa
6 cups flour
6 cups sugar
1 1/2 cups sour cream
6 eggs
1 tablespoon baking soda
1 tablespoon vanilla extract
1 1/2 teaspoons salt
Chocolate Icing

Bring the margarine, water and baking cocoa to a boil in a saucepan. Cool. Stir in the flour, sugar, sour cream, eggs, baking soda, vanilla and salt. Spoon into a large sheet cake pan. Bake at 400 degrees for 20 minutes. Spread with Chocolate Icing. *Yield: 16 to 24 servings.*

Chocolate Icing

1 1/2 cups margarine
1 cup plus 1 tablespoon milk
3/4 cup baking cocoa
3 (1-pound) packages confectioners' sugar
1 tablespoon vanilla extract

Boil the margarine, milk and baking cocoa in a saucepan. Cool. Beat the chocolate mixture and confectioners' sugar in a mixer bowl until of spreading consistency. Stir in the vanilla.

Mary Rogers

Yeast Chocolate Cake

1 cake yeast or 1 envelope dry yeast	1 cup butter or margarine, softened	1 cup milk, scalded, cooled
¼ cup lukewarm water	2 cups sugar	1 teaspoon baking soda
3¾ cups flour	3 eggs	3 tablespoons hot water
1 teaspoon salt	3 ounces unsweetened chocolate, melted	2 teaspoons vanilla extract

Dissolve the yeast in the lukewarm water. Let stand for 5 minutes. Sift the flour and salt into a bowl and mix well. Beat the butter in a mixer bowl until creamy. Add the sugar, beating until blended. Add the eggs. Beat until light and fluffy, scraping the bowl occasionally. Stir in the chocolate. Add ⅓ of the dry ingredients to the creamed mixture and mix well. Stir in the yeast mixture and ½ of the milk. Add ½ of the remaining dry ingredients and the remaining ½ cup milk. Beat until smooth. Stir in the remaining dry ingredients. Let stand, covered, in a cool place overnight.

Dissolve the baking soda in the hot water in a bowl and mix well. Stir in the vanilla. Stir into the batter. Spoon into 3 greased 9-inch cake pans. Let stand in a warm place for 25 minutes. Bake at 350 degrees for 30 minutes or until the layers test done. Cool in the pans for several minutes. Invert onto a wire rack to cool completely. Frost with your favorite chocolate or white frosting. *Yield: 12 servings.*

Jessie Joy

St. Fanny Cake

1 teaspoon baking soda	1 cup raisins	¼ teaspoon nutmeg
½ cup warm water	½ cup butter or lard	2 cups flour
1 cup sugar	1 teaspoon cinnamon	½ teaspoon baking powder
1 cup cold water	½ teaspoon each ground cloves and salt	

Dissolve the baking soda in the warm water. Combine the sugar, cold water, raisins, butter, cinnamon, cloves, salt and nutmeg in a saucepan. Bring to a boil. Boil for 5 minutes, stirring frequently. Remove from heat. Stir in the baking soda mixture, flour and baking powder. Spoon into a cake pan. Bake at 350 degrees for 40 minutes. *Yield: 15 servings.*

Barbara Smith

Chop Suey Cake

2 cups flour	1 (20-ounce) can juice-	1 cup chopped nuts
2 cups sugar	pack crushed pineapple	Cream Cheese Frosting
2 teaspoons baking soda	2 eggs	1/4 cup chopped nuts

Combine the flour, sugar, baking soda, undrained pineapple and eggs in a mixer bowl. Beat until mixed, scraping the bowl occasionally. Stir in 1 cup nuts. Spoon into a greased 9x13-inch cake pan. Bake at 350 degrees for 40 to 45 minutes or until the cake tests done. Spread with the Cream Cheese Frosting. Sprinkle with 1/4 cup nuts. Yield: 15 servings.

Cream Cheese Frosting

1/2 cup margarine, softened	1 1/2 teaspoons vanilla	2 cups confectioners'
4 ounces cream cheese	extract	sugar

Beat the margarine, softened cream cheese and vanilla in a mixer bowl until light and fluffy. Add the confectioners' sugar gradually, beating constantly until of spreading consistency.

Thelma O'Brien

Craters-of-the-Moon Cake

1 1/2 cups sifted flour	1 teaspoon salt	1 teaspoon vanilla extract
1/2 cup sugar	1 teaspoon baking soda	1 teaspoon white vinegar
1/2 cup packed brown sugar	5 tablespoons melted butter	1 cup milk
1/4 cup baking cocoa		2/3 cup miniature marshmallows

Mix the flour, sugar, brown sugar, baking cocoa and salt in a 9-inch cake pan; you now have light brown moon sand. Make a big crater with a spoon in the center of the mixture, exposing the bottom of the pan. Make a medium-size crater on 1 side and a smaller crater on the other side. Spoon the baking soda into the medium-size crater, the melted butter into the large crater and the vanilla into the smallest crater. Pour the vinegar into the medium-size crater; watch how it becomes a bubbling volcano. Pour the milk over the top of the moon sand when the bubbles cease and mix gently. Sprinkle with the marshmallows. Bake at 350 degrees for 35 minutes or until the cake tests done. Cool. *Yield: 12 servings.*

Lornie Porter

Fruitcakes

5 pounds fruitcake mix (chopped citron, lemon peel, orange peel, candied cherries and pineapple)
3 pounds seedless raisins
3 pounds seeded raisins
1 package dates, chopped
1/2 package figs, chopped
4 ounces chopped walnuts
4 ounces chopped pecans
4 ounces slivered almonds
1 1/2 cups orange marmalade
3/4 cup lemon juice
3/4 cup orange juice
1/2 cup red wine
2 teaspoons grated lemon peel
1 1/2 teaspoons vanilla extract
1 1/2 teaspoons lemon extract
6 cups sifted flour
1 tablespoon cinnamon
1 1/2 teaspoons nutmeg
1 1/2 teaspoons salt
1 1/2 teaspoons baking powder
1/2 teaspoon baking soda
1/4 teaspoon ground cloves
3 cups butter, softened
3 cups sugar
18 eggs

Combine the fruitcake mix, raisins, dates, figs, walnuts, pecans and almonds in a large bowl and mix well. Add a mixture of the marmalade, lemon juice, orange juice, wine, lemon peel and flavorings and mix well. Let stand, covered, in a moderately warm place overnight. Sift the flour, cinnamon, nutmeg, salt, baking powder, baking soda and cloves 3 times. Beat the butter and sugar in a mixer bowl until light and fluffy. Add the eggs 1 at a time, beating well after each addition. Add the dry ingredients gradually, beating well after each addition. Stir in the fruit mixture. Fill cake pans to within 1/2 inch of the top edge.

Place a pan of water on the bottom oven rack. Place the fruitcakes on the middle oven rack. Bake at 250 degrees for 4 to 5 hours or until the fruitcakes test done. If your oven is not large enough to bake all the fruitcakes at once, store the batter, covered with foil, in the refrigerator until just before baking. *Yield: 16 pounds.*

Sara Chambers

Very Best Fruitcakes

1 1/2 cups flour
1 teaspoon salt
1 teaspoon baking powder
1 teaspoon allspice
1/2 teaspoon nutmeg
1/2 teaspoon ground cloves
1 1/2 pounds candied cherries, cut into halves

8 ounces seeded raisins
8 ounces dates, cut into halves
8 ounces candied pineapple, chopped
4 ounces citron
4 ounces lemon peel
4 ounces orange peel

4 ounces walnut halves
4 ounces pecan halves
1/4 cup flour
1 cup shortening
1/2 cup sugar
1/2 cup honey
5 eggs, beaten
6 tablespoons orange juice

Line 2 greased cake pans with waxed paper, allowing a 1/2-inch overhang. Sift 1 1/2 cups flour, salt, baking powder, allspice, nutmeg and cloves into a bowl and mix well. Combine the cherries, raisins, dates, pineapple, citron, lemon peel, orange peel, walnuts and pecans in a large bowl and mix well. Add 1/4 cup flour, tossing to coat. Beat the shortening and sugar in a mixer bowl until creamy, scraping the bowl occasionally. Add the honey and eggs, beating until blended. Add the flour mixture alternately with the orange juice, beating well after each addition. Pour over the fruit mixture and mix well. Spoon the batter into the prepared pans; do not flatten.

Place a baking pan filled with 2 cups water on the bottom oven rack. Bake the fruitcakes on the middle oven rack at 250 degrees for 3 to 4 hours or until the cakes test done. The water causes the fruitcakes to have a greater volume, a moister texture and a smooth shiny surface. Remove to a wire rack to cool. Wrap the fruitcakes in rum-soaked cheesecloth; cover with foil. *Yield: 5 pounds.*

Alice Sawyer

Old-Fashioned Jelly Roll

4 eggs
¾ teaspoon baking powder
¼ teaspoon salt
¾ cup sugar
¾ cup flour, sifted
1 teaspoon vanilla extract
Confectioners' sugar
Jelly

Line a greased 10x15-inch jelly roll pan with waxed paper. Grease the waxed paper. Combine the eggs, baking powder and salt in a bowl and mix well. Place the bowl over a smaller bowl filled with hot water. Add the sugar gradually, beating constantly with a rotary beater until thickened and pale yellow. Remove the bowl from the hot water. Fold in the flour and vanilla. Spread in the prepared pan. Bake at 400 degrees for 13 minutes. Trim the crusty edges. Invert the cake onto a tea towel sprinkled with confectioners' sugar. Remove the waxed paper. Spread jelly almost to the edge; roll to enclose the filling. Wrap in a tea towel. Let stand on a wire rack until cool. *Yield: 12 to 16 servings.*

Ruth Clark

Hawaiian Cake

2 cups flour
2 cups sugar
2 teaspoons baking soda
2 cups drained crushed pineapple
2 eggs, beaten
1 cup chopped walnuts
Vanilla Frosting

Mix the flour, sugar and baking soda in a bowl. Stir in the pineapple, eggs and walnuts. Spoon into a greased and floured 9x13-inch cake pan. Bake at 350 degrees for 40 minutes. Cool in the pan on a wire rack. Spread with the Vanilla Frosting. *Yield: 15 servings.*

Vanilla Frosting

8 ounces cream cheese, softened
½ cup butter, softened
1 tablespoon vanilla extract
1½ to 2 cups confectioners' sugar

Beat the cream cheese and butter in a mixer bowl until creamy, scraping the bowl occasionally. Add the vanilla, beating until blended. Add the confectioners' sugar gradually, beating constantly until of spreading consistency.

Rosemary Lounsbury

Mackinac Sailing Cake

1 3/4 cups flour
1 teaspoon baking powder
1/4 teaspoon baking soda
1/4 teaspoon salt
8 ounces cream cheese, softened

1/2 cup margarine, softened
1 1/4 cups sugar
2 eggs
1 teaspoon vanilla extract

1/4 cup milk
1 1/2 cups flour
3/4 cup sugar
10 tablespoons unsalted butter, chilled

Sift 1 3/4 cups flour, baking powder, baking soda and salt into a bowl and mix well. Beat the cream cheese and margarine in a mixer bowl until creamy, scraping the bowl occasionally. Beat in 1 1/4 cups sugar, eggs and vanilla until blended. Add the dry ingredients alternately with the milk, beating well after each addition. Spoon into a greased and floured 9x13-inch cake pan. Combine 1 1/2 cups flour and 3/4 cup sugar in a bowl and mix well. Cut in the butter until crumbly. Sprinkle over the prepared layer. Bake at 350 degrees for 30 to 45 minutes or until light golden brown. *Yield: 15 servings.*

Ilse Schmitt

Mayonnaise Cake

2 cups flour
1 cup sugar

1/4 cup baking cocoa
2 teaspoons baking soda
1 cup water

1 cup mayonnaise
1 teaspoon vanilla extract

Combine the flour, sugar, baking cocoa and baking soda in a bowl and mix well. Stir in the water, mayonnaise and vanilla. Spoon into a greased 9x13-inch cake pan. Bake at 325 degrees until the cake tests done. *Yield: 15 servings.*

Louann Mosley

Mississippi Mud Cake

2 cups sugar
1 cup margarine
1½ cups flour
4 eggs, beaten

2 tablespoons baking cocoa
1 tablespoon vanilla extract
1 cup chopped walnuts

3 cups miniature marshmallows or marshmallow creme
Mississippi Mud Frosting

Combine the sugar and margarine in a saucepan. Heat until the margarine melts and the sugar dissolves, stirring constantly. Remove from heat. Add the flour and mix well. Stir in the eggs. Add the baking cocoa, vanilla and walnuts and mix well. Spread in a greased and floured 9x13-inch cake pan. Bake at 375 degrees for 25 to 30 minutes. Remove from oven. Sprinkle with the marshmallows. Let stand, covered with foil, for 5 to 10 minutes or until the marshmallows begin to soften; spread evenly with a knife. Let stand until cool. Top with Mississippi Mud Frosting. *Yield: 15 servings.*

Mississippi Mud Frosting

6 tablespoons margarine, softened
¼ cup milk

2 cups confectioners' sugar
2 tablespoons plus 2 teaspoons baking cocoa

½ teaspoon vanilla extract

Beat the margarine in a mixer bowl until creamy. Add the milk, confectioners' sugar, baking cocoa and vanilla, beating constantly until of spreading consistency.

Joanne Zwolinski

Orange Cake

2 cups sugar
1 cup margarine or shortening
4 eggs
1 1/3 cups sour milk
2 teaspoons (heaping) baking soda
4 cups sifted flour
2 teaspoons vanilla extract
Grated peel and juice of 4 to 6 oranges
2 cups raisins
1 cup chopped nuts
1 cup sugar

Beat 2 cups sugar and margarine in a mixer bowl until creamy. Beat in the eggs 1 at a time. Add a mixture of the sour milk and baking soda and mix well. Stir in the flour and vanilla. Fold in the orange peel. Stir in the raisins and nuts. Spoon into an angel food cake pan. Bake at 375 degrees for 60 to 70 minutes or until the cake tests done. Remove to a serving plate. Combine the orange juice and 1 cup sugar in a saucepan. Heat until the sugar dissolves, stirring frequently. Pour over the hot cake. Let stand until cool. *Yield: 16 servings.*

Irene Gates

Poppy Seed Cake

3/4 cup poppy seeds
1/2 cup milk
1 cup sugar
1/2 cup butter, softened
1/2 cup milk
2 1/4 cups cake flour
2 teaspoons baking powder
1 teaspoon vanilla extract
4 egg whites, stiffly beaten
Custard Filling

Soak the poppy seeds in 1/2 cup milk in a bowl overnight. Beat the sugar and butter in a mixer bowl until creamy. Add 1/2 cup milk alternately with a mixture of the cake flour and baking powder, mixing well after each addition. Stir in the vanilla and poppy seed mixture. Fold in the egg whites. Spoon into 2 cake pans. Bake at 350 degrees until the layers test done. Cool on a wire rack. Spread the Custard Filling between the layers. *Yield: 12 servings.*

Custard Filling

1 cup milk, scalded
3/4 cup sugar
1 tablespoon flour
Salt to taste
4 egg yolks, beaten

Combine the milk, sugar, flour and salt in a double boiler and mix well. Stir in the egg yolks. Cook over low heat for 3 minutes, stirring frequently. Let stand until cool.

Catherine Nordberg

Grandma Libby's Pumpkin Cake

1 1/2 cups flour
1 teaspoon baking soda
1 teaspoon baking powder
1 teaspoon cinnamon
1/2 teaspoon salt
1 cup sugar
1 cup pumpkin
3/4 cup vegetable oil
2 eggs
Butter Frosting

Combine the flour, baking soda, baking powder, cinnamon and salt in a bowl and mix well. Combine the sugar, pumpkin, oil and eggs in a bowl and mix well. Add to the dry ingredients, stirring until blended. Spoon into an ungreased tube pan. Bake at 350 degrees for 35 to 40 minutes or until the cake tests done. Spread with the Butter Frosting. *Yield: 16 servings.*

Butter Frosting

1/2 cup butter or margarine, softened
1 egg
1 teaspoon vanilla extract
3 1/2 to 4 cups confectioners' sugar

Beat the butter, egg and vanilla in a mixer bowl until smooth. Add the confectioners' sugar gradually, beating constantly until of a spreading consistency.

Alice Martin

Rhubarb Cake

4 cups finely chopped rhubarb
1 cup sugar
1 (3-ounce) package strawberry gelatin
1 cup miniature marshmallows
1 (2-layer) package white cake mix

Combine the rhubarb, sugar, gelatin and marshmallows in a bowl and mix well. Spoon into a greased and floured 9x13-inch cake pan. Prepare the cake mix using package directions. Spread over the prepared layer. Bake at 350 degrees for 35 to 40 minutes or until the cake tests done. *Yield: 15 servings.*

Marilyn Wilkins

Sock-It-To-Me Cake

1 (2-layer) package butter- and pudding-recipe cake mix
2 cups sour cream
¾ cup vegetable oil
½ cup sugar
4 eggs
3 tablespoons brown sugar
1 tablespoon cinnamon

Combine the cake mix, sour cream, oil, sugar, eggs, brown sugar and cinnamon in a bowl and mix well. Spoon into a bundt pan. Bake at 350 degrees for 1 hour. *Yield: 16 servings.*

Gracie Koerbel

Pineapple Torte

¾ cup sugar
3 tablespoons cornstarch
2 (20-ounce) cans crushed pineapple
2½ cups flour, sifted
1 teaspoon baking powder
½ teaspoon baking soda
½ teaspoon salt
1 cup corn oil
1 cup sugar
4 eggs
1 teaspoon vanilla extract

Combine ¾ cup sugar and cornstarch in a saucepan and mix well. Stir in the undrained pineapple. Cook until thickened, stirring constantly. Let stand until cool. Sift the flour, baking powder, baking soda and salt twice. Beat the oil and 1 cup sugar in a mixer bowl until blended. Add the eggs 1 at a time, beating well after each addition. Add the vanilla and dry ingredients and mix well.

Spread ¾ of the batter into a greased 11x17-inch cake pan. Top with the pineapple mixture. Drop the remaining batter by spoonfuls over the top and swirl with a knife. Bake at 350 degrees for 30 to 35 minutes or until the torte tests done. May sprinkle with confectioners' sugar while warm or serve with whipped cream or vanilla ice cream.
Yield: 18 servings.

Selma Dufina

Butter Sponge Cake

2 1/4 cups cake flour
2 teaspoons baking powder
11 egg yolks

2 cups sugar
1 cup milk, scalded, cooled
1 teaspoon vanilla extract

1/2 cup melted butter
Lemon Filling
Marshmallow Frosting

Sift the cake flour and baking powder into a bowl and mix well. Beat the egg yolks in a mixer bowl until thickened and pale yellow. Add the sugar gradually, beating constantly until light and fluffy. Stir in the milk and vanilla gradually. Fold in the dry ingredients. Add the butter and mix gently. Spoon into 2 waxed-paper-lined 9-inch cake pans. Bake at 350 degrees for 50 minutes. Remove to a wire rack to cool. Place 1 of the cake layers on a cake plate. Spread with the Lemon Filling. Top with the remaining cake layer. Spread the Marshmallow Frosting over the top and side of the cake. *Yield: 12 servings.*

Lemon Filling

1 cup sugar
3 tablespoons cornstarch

1/2 teaspoon salt
1 cup water
1/2 cup lemon juice

2 tablespoons butter
4 egg yolks, lightly beaten

Combine the sugar, cornstarch and salt in a saucepan and mix well. Add the water, lemon juice and butter. Bring to a rolling boil. Boil for 1 minute, stirring frequently. Stir a small amount of the hot mixture into the egg yolks; stir the egg yolks into the hot mixture.

Marshmallow Frosting

1 cup sugar
1/3 cup water

1 tablespoon light corn syrup

13 marshmallows
2 egg whites, stiffly beaten

Combine the sugar, water and corn syrup in a saucepan and mix well. Cook to 234 to 240 degrees on a candy thermometer, soft-ball stage. Stir in the marshmallows. Pour over the egg whites in a mixer bowl. Beat until fluffy. May substitute the equivalent amount of marshmallow creme for the marshmallows.

Margaret Doud

Yuletide Cake

1 (8-ounce) jar maraschino cherries, drained
8 ounces pitted whole dates
1/2 cup seedless raisins
1/2 cup seedless yellow currants (optional)
1 1/2 cups whole almonds
1 1/2 cups walnut halves
3/4 cup flour
3/4 cup sugar
1/2 teaspoon salt
1/2 teaspoon baking powder
3 eggs
1 tablespoon brandy or rum extract

Combine the cherries, dates, raisins, currants, almonds and walnuts in a bowl and mix well. Sift the flour, sugar, salt and baking powder into a bowl and mix well. Add to the fruit and nut mixture and mix well. Beat the eggs in a mixer bowl until light and fluffy. Stir in the brandy flavoring. Add to the fruit and nut batter and mix well. Spoon into a greased and floured 5x9-inch cake pan or round cake pan; press firmly. Bake at 300 degrees for 1 1/2 hours or until golden brown. Cool in the pan on a wire rack for 10 minutes. Invert onto a wire rack to cool completely. *Yield: 12 servings.*

Linda D. Horn

Busy-Day Icing

2 cups sifted confectioners' sugar
1/3 cup shortening
2 ounces chocolate, melted
1 egg
1/3 teaspoon salt

Combine the confectioners' sugar, shortening, chocolate, egg and salt in a mixer bowl. Beat until fluffy, scraping the bowl occasionally. To avoid raw eggs that may carry salmonella we suggest using an equivalent amount of commercial egg substitute. *Yield: 1 1/2 cups.*

Thelma O'Brien

Creamy Nut Frosting

½ cup milk
2½ tablespoons flour
½ cup sugar

¼ cup shortening
¼ cup butter, softened
½ teaspoon vanilla extract

½ cup chopped nuts
1 cup confectioners' sugar

Add the milk gradually to the flour in a saucepan and mix well. Cook until thickened or of the consistency of a paste, stirring constantly. Beat the sugar, shortening and butter in a mixer bowl until creamy. Add the flour mixture and vanilla. Beat until fluffy. Stir in the nuts. Use ⅓ of the mixture for a filling. Blend 1 cup confectioners' sugar with the remaining mixture and spread over the top and side of a cake. *Yield: 1½ cups.*

Marilyn McCready

Lemon Butter Icing

2 tablespoons butter or margarine, softened
1½ tablespoons milk
1 tablespoon lemon juice

1 teaspoon grated lemon peel
⅛ teaspoon salt
2 cups sifted confectioners' sugar

Milk (optional)
Yellow food coloring (optional)

Combine the butter, 1½ tablespoons milk, lemon juice, lemon peel and salt in a mixer bowl and beat well. Add the confectioners' sugar, beating until smooth and fluffy. May add a few drops of milk for the desired consistency. Blend in food coloring if desired. *Yield: 1½ cups.*

Marilyn McCready

Quick Icing

5 tablespoons brown sugar

3 tablespoons butter, softened

2 tablespoons cream
½ cup chopped nuts

Combine the brown sugar, butter and cream in a bowl and mix well. Stir in the nuts. Spread on a warm cake. Broil until brown and bubbly. *Yield: ½ cup.*

Marilyn Wilkins

Aunt Nonie's Frosting

1 cup milk
3 tablespoons flour
½ cup shortening
½ cup margarine, softened
1 cup sugar
1 teaspoon vanilla extract

Combine the milk and flour in a saucepan and mix well. Cook until thickened, stirring constantly. Let stand until cool. Beat the shortening and margarine in a mixer bowl for 4 minutes, scraping the bowl occasionally. Stir in the flour mixture. Beat for 4 minutes. Add the sugar and vanilla. Beat for 4 minutes longer, scraping the bowl occasionally. Frost a 2-layer cake or 2 sheet cakes. Add 1 envelope chocolate syrup for baking and cooking to make chocolate frosting. *Yield: 1½ cups.*

Barbara Fisher

Swirl Frosting

½ cup sugar
½ cup light corn syrup
2 egg whites
¼ teaspoon cream of tartar
⅛ teaspoon salt
Vanilla extract to taste

Combine the sugar and corn syrup in a saucepan. Cook over medium heat until the sugar dissolves and bubbles appear around the edge of the pan, stirring occasionally. Beat the egg whites, cream of tartar and salt in a mixer bowl until almost stiff. Pour the hot syrup in a thin stream over the egg whites, beating constantly at high speed until stiff peaks form. Stir in the vanilla. *Yield: 3 cups.*

Mrs. B. C. Morse, Jr.

Fluffy Uncooked Frosting

1 cup sugar
½ cup boiling water
1 egg white
1 teaspoon vanilla extract
¼ teaspoon cream of tartar

Combine the sugar, boiling water, egg white, vanilla and cream of tartar in a mixer bowl. Beat at high speed for 5 minutes or until stiff, scraping the bowl occasionally. *Yield: 1½ cups.*

Lura Albee

Aggression Cookies

1½ cups packed brown sugar
3 cups quick-cooking oats
1½ cups margarine or butter, softened
1½ teaspoons baking soda
1½ cups sifted flour

Combine the brown sugar, oats, margarine, baking soda and flour in the order listed in a bowl and mix well. Shape into 1-inch balls. Arrange 3 inches apart on an ungreased cookie sheet. Flatten with the bottom of a glass coated with butter and dipped in sugar. Bake at 350 degrees for 10 minutes or until golden brown. Cool on the cookie sheet for 2 to 3 minutes. Remove to a wire rack to cool completely. *Yield: 2 dozen cookies.*

Lornie Porter

Angel Cookies

1 cup shortening
1 cup butter, softened
1 cup packed light brown sugar
1 cup sugar
2 eggs
2 teaspoons vanilla extract
4 cups flour
2 teaspoons baking soda
2 teaspoons cream of tartar

Beat the shortening, butter, brown sugar and sugar in a mixer bowl until creamy. Add the eggs and vanilla, beating until blended. Add a sifted mixture of the flour, baking soda and cream of tartar and mix well. Drop by teaspoonfuls onto a nonstick cookie sheet. Bake at 375 degrees for 12 to 15 minutes or until light brown. Cool on the cookie sheet for 2 minutes. Remove to a wire rack to cool completely. *Yield: 4 dozen cookies.*

Florence McIntyre

Chocolate Chip Biscotti

2 cups flour
1/2 teaspoon baking soda
1/4 teaspoon salt
1/2 cup sugar
1/2 cup packed brown sugar
2 eggs, at room temperature
1 teaspoon vanilla extract
1 cup miniature chocolate chips
1/2 cup chopped pecans

Line 2 cookie sheets with parchment paper or foil. Mix the flour, baking soda and salt in a bowl. Combine the sugar, brown sugar and eggs in a mixer bowl. Beat at high speed until thick and pale yellow, scraping the bowl occasionally. Add the vanilla, beating until blended. Add the dry ingredients. Beat at low speed just until moistened. Stir in the chocolate chips and pecans.

Divide the dough into 3 equal portions. Shape each portion into a 12-inch log. Arrange the logs 3 inches apart on prepared cookie sheets. Smooth and flatten the top of each log slightly. Bake at 350 degrees for 30 minutes or until firm to the touch; the logs will begin to crack. Place the cookie sheets on a wire rack. Loosen the logs with a spatula. Let stand for 10 minutes.

Reduce the oven temperature to 325 degrees. Place the logs on a cutting board. Cut each log diagonally into 1/2-inch slices with a serrated knife. Arrange cut side down on cookie sheets. Bake for 7 to 8 minutes; turn. Bake for 7 to 8 minutes longer or until dry and crisp. Remove to a wire rack to cool.

Store in an airtight container at room temperature for up to 1 month or freeze for up to 3 months. For variety, substitute 1 teaspoon almond extract for the vanilla and 1 1/2 cups thinly sliced almonds for the chocolate chips and pecans. Bake as directed. Dip 1/4 to 1/2 of each slice into melted baking chocolate. Let stand until set. *Yield: 6 dozen.*

Linda D. Horn

Chocolate Squares

2 ounces chocolate
1/2 cup butter, softened
2 eggs
1 cup sugar
1/2 teaspoon baking powder
3/4 cup flour
1 teaspoon vanilla extract
1 cup chopped pecans

Heat the chocolate in a double boiler until melted, stirring frequently. Add the butter and mix well. Remove from heat. Beat the eggs in a mixer bowl until foamy. Add the sugar, baking powder and flour and mix well. Stir in the chocolate mixture. Add the vanilla and pecans and mix well. Spread in a baking pan. Bake at 375 degrees for 15 minutes. Let stand until cool. Cut into squares. *Yield: 1 dozen squares.*

Helen Puttkammer

Bourbon Balls

3 cups finely crushed vanilla wafer crumbs
1 cup finely chopped pecans

1 cup confectioners' sugar
1/2 cup baking cocoa
1/2 cup bourbon
3 tablespoons corn syrup

Confectioners' sugar, baking cocoa or shredded coconut to taste

Combine the vanilla wafer crumbs, pecans, 1 cup confectioners' sugar, 1/2 cup baking cocoa, bourbon and corn syrup in a bowl and mix well. Shape into balls. Roll the balls in confectioners' sugar to taste, baking cocoa to taste or shredded coconut. May substitute rum for the bourbon. *Yield: 2 dozen.*

Grandma's Kitchen

Brownies

2 cups flour
2 cups sugar
1 teaspoon baking soda
1/2 teaspoon salt

1 cup margarine
1 cup water
3 tablespoons baking cocoa

1/2 cup milk
2 eggs, beaten
1 teaspoon vanilla extract
Chocolate Frosting

Mix the flour, sugar, baking soda and salt in a bowl. Bring the margarine, water and baking cocoa to a boil in a saucepan, stirring frequently. Stir into the flour mixture. Cool slightly. Add the milk, eggs and vanilla and mix well. Spoon into a 9x13-inch baking pan. Bake at 350 degrees for 20 to 25 minutes or until the brownies test done. Cool in the pan on a wire rack. Spread with the Chocolate Frosting. Cut into bars. *Yield: 3 dozen bars.*

Chocolate Frosting

1 1/2 cups sugar

1/2 cup margarine
6 tablespoons milk

2/3 cup chocolate chips

Bring the sugar, margarine and milk to a boil in a saucepan. Boil for 30 seconds, stirring frequently. Remove from heat. Add the chocolate chips, stirring until blended. Let stand until cool.

Christine McCready

Rocky Road Brownies

2/3 cup butter
2 ounces unsweetened chocolate
2 cups sugar
2 teaspoons vanilla extract
4 eggs
1 1/2 cups flour
1 teaspoon baking powder
1 1/2 cups chopped nuts
Miniature marshmallows
Chocolate Glaze

Melt the butter and chocolate in a saucepan over low heat, stirring constantly. Combine the chocolate mixture, sugar and vanilla in a mixer bowl. Beat until smooth. Add the eggs, beating until blended. Add a sifted mixture of the flour and baking powder and mix well. Stir in the nuts. Spread in a greased 9x13-inch baking pan. Bake at 350 degrees for 35 to 40 minutes or until the brownies test done. Sprinkle marshmallows over the baked layer. Bake for 3 to 4 minutes longer or until the marshmallows are light brown. Drizzle with the Chocolate Glaze. Let stand until set. Cut into bars. *Yield: 3 dozen bars.*

Chocolate Glaze

3 ounces unsweetened chocolate
1/4 cup butter
3 cups sifted confectioners' sugar
1 1/2 teaspoons vanilla extract
Hot water

Heat the chocolate and butter in a saucepan over low heat until melted, stirring constantly. Remove from heat. Add the confectioners' sugar and vanilla, stirring until crumbly. Add hot water until of drizzling consistency and mix well.

Florence McIntyre

Delightful Cookies

12 (4-section) graham crackers
1 cup margarine
1/2 cup sugar
Chopped walnuts to taste
8 ounces milk chocolate, melted

Break each graham cracker into 4 portions along the perforations. Arrange on a nonstick cookie sheet. Bring the margarine and sugar to a boil in a saucepan. Boil for 3 minutes, stirring constantly. Pour over the graham crackers; sprinkle with the walnuts. Bake at 325 degrees for 10 minutes. Remove to a sheet of waxed paper. Drizzle with the chocolate. Cool. *Yield: 4 dozen cookies.*

Laura Eiseler

Fruit Squares

1 cup boiling water
½ cup dried apricots
½ cup prunes
2 teaspoons lemon juice
½ teaspoon salt
½ cup shortening
½ cup sugar
1½ cups quick-cooking oats
1 cup sifted flour
3 tablespoons molasses

Combine the boiling water, apricots, prunes, lemon juice and salt in a saucepan. Cook for 5 minutes, stirring occasionally. Let stand until cool. Beat the shortening and sugar in a mixer bowl until creamy, scraping the bowl occasionally. Stir in the oats, flour and molasses. Press ½ of the oat mixture into an 8x8-inch baking pan. Spread the apricot mixture over the prepared layer. Press the remaining oat mixture over the top. Bake at 375 degrees for 25 minutes. Let stand until cool. Cut into squares. *Yield: 2 dozen squares.*

Mary Kate McGreevy

Old-Fashioned Ginger Cookies

1 cup molasses
1 cup packed brown sugar
1 cup shortening
1 cup cold strong coffee
1 tablespoon vanilla extract
1 teaspoon baking soda
1 teaspoon salt
1 teaspoon ginger
Flour
Sugar to taste

Combine the molasses, brown sugar, shortening, coffee, vanilla, baking soda, salt and ginger in a mixer bowl. Beat until blended, scraping the bowl occasionally. Add just enough flour to make a dough that can be rolled easily. Chill, covered, in the refrigerator. Roll the dough thin on a lightly floured surface; cut with a cookie cutter. Arrange on a nonstick cookie sheet. Sprinkle with sugar. Bake at 350 degrees until brown. Cool on the cookie sheet for 2 minutes. Remove to a wire rack to cool completely. *Yield: 2 to 3 dozen cookies.*

Nan Rudolph

Galettes or French Cakes

2 cups butter, softened
4 1/2 cups flour
3 cups sugar
6 eggs
1/8 teaspoon baking soda

Beat the butter until creamy in a mixer bowl. Add the flour, sugar, eggs and baking soda and mix well. Bake in a waffle iron until golden brown using manufacturer's directions; 1 tablespoon of the batter makes 1 cake. Serve plain or with a dessert sauce of choice.
Yield: variable.

Mrs. Melvin Fuelling

Irish Cookies

3/4 cup packed dark brown sugar
1/2 cup butter or margarine, softened
1 egg
2 teaspoons vanilla extract
2 cups flour
3 tablespoons Irish cream
3/4 teaspoon baking soda
1/4 teaspoon salt
1 to 2 cups chocolate chunks
1/2 cup chopped nuts (optional)

Combine the brown sugar, butter, egg and vanilla in a mixer bowl. Beat until fluffy, scraping the bowl occasionally. Add the flour, Irish cream, baking soda and salt, beating until blended. Stir in the chocolate chunks and nuts. Shape into 1-inch balls. Arrange on a lightly greased cookie sheet. Bake at 350 degrees for 8 to 10 minutes or until light brown. Cool on the cookie sheet for 2 minutes. Remove to a wire rack to cool completely.
Yield: 2 to 3 dozen cookies.

McNally Cottage

Lemon Squares

1 cup flour
1/4 cup confectioners' sugar
1/8 teaspoon salt
1/2 cup butter, softened
1 cup sugar
4 to 5 tablespoons lemon juice
2 tablespoons flour
1/2 teaspoon baking powder
2 eggs

Process the flour, confectioners' sugar, salt and butter in a food processor until crumbly. Pat over the bottom of an ungreased 8x8-inch baking pan. Bake at 325 degrees for 15 minutes. Combine the sugar and lemon juice in a bowl, stirring until the sugar dissolves. Stir in the flour, baking powder and eggs and mix well. Spoon over the baked layer. Bake for 25 to 30 minutes. Let stand until cool. Cut into squares. *Yield: 2 dozen squares.*

Kathleen Hoppenrath

Lizzies

1/2 cup flour
1 teaspoon cinnamon
1/4 teaspoon nutmeg
1/4 teaspoon ground cloves
1 1/2 cups packed brown sugar
1/4 cup butter or margarine, softened
2 eggs, beaten
1 (1-pound) package seeded raisins
1 cup flour
1/4 cup bourbon
1/4 cup orange juice
1 1/2 tablespoons milk
16 ounces pecan halves
16 ounces candied cherries
8 ounces citron, chopped

Sift 1/2 cup flour, cinnamon, nutmeg and cloves into a bowl and mix well. Beat the brown sugar and butter in a mixer bowl until creamy, scraping the bowl occasionally. Add the eggs, beating until blended. Add the sifted ingredients and mix well. Combine the raisins and 1 cup flour in a bowl, tossing to coat. Stir in the bourbon, orange juice and milk. Add the raisin mixture, pecans, cherries and citron to the creamed mixture and mix well. Drop by teaspoonfuls onto a greased cookie sheet. Bake at 325 degrees for 25 minutes. Cool on the cookie sheet for 2 minutes. Remove to a wire rack to cool completely.
Yield: 3 to 4 dozen cookies.

Catherine McNally

Mincemeat Hermits

1 1/2 cups flour
2 teaspoons cinnamon
1 teaspoon baking powder
1/2 teaspoon salt
1/4 teaspoon baking soda
1 cup packed brown sugar
2/3 cup shortening
1 egg
2 cups quick-cooking oats
1 1/2 cups mincemeat

Sift the flour, cinnamon, baking powder, salt and baking soda into a bowl and mix well. Beat the brown sugar and shortening in a mixer bowl until creamy. Stir in the egg, oats and mincemeat. Add the flour mixture and mix well. Drop by teaspoonfuls onto a greased cookie sheet. Bake at 350 degrees for 15 to 17 minutes or until light brown.
Yield: 2 to 3 dozen cookies.

Florence Vance

Peanut Butter Oatmeal Cookies

2 teaspoons baking soda
2 tablespoons hot water
1 cup sugar
1 cup packed brown sugar
1 cup shortening
1 cup peanut butter
2 eggs
1 teaspoon vanilla extract
5 cups rolled oats
1/2 cup flour
1/2 teaspoon salt

Dissolve the baking soda in the hot water in a small bowl and mix well. Beat the sugar, brown sugar, shortening and peanut butter in a mixer bowl until creamy, scraping the bowl occasionally. Add the eggs and baking soda mixture and mix well. Beat in the vanilla. Stir in the oats, flour and salt. Shape into 1-inch balls. Arrange on a nonstick cookie sheet; press lightly with a floured fork. Bake at 350 degrees for 10 to 12 minutes or until golden brown. Cool on the cookie sheet for 2 minutes. Remove to a wire rack to cool completely.
Yield: 2 to 3 dozen cookies.

Elizabeth Sieffert

Oatmeal Refrigerator Cookies

1 cup shortening
1 cup sugar
1 cup packed brown sugar
2 eggs
1 teaspoon vanilla extract
1½ cups flour
1 teaspoon baking soda
1 teaspoon salt
3 cups rolled oats

Beat the shortening, sugar and brown sugar in a mixer bowl until creamy. Add the eggs, beating until blended. Beat in the vanilla. Add a mixture of the flour, baking soda and salt and mix well. Stir in the oats. Shape into a log 2½ inches in diameter. Chill, wrapped in waxed paper, for several hours to overnight. Cut into slices. Place on an ungreased cookie sheet. Bake at 350 to 375 degrees for 11 to 12 minutes or until light brown.
Yield: 5 dozen cookies.

Barbara Beal Libby

Ozark Cookies

⅔ cup sugar
1 egg
2 tablespoons flour
1½ teaspoons baking powder
⅛ teaspoon salt
½ cup chopped apple
½ cup chopped nuts
1 teaspoon vanilla extract

Beat the sugar and egg in a mixer bowl until smooth. Stir in a mixture of the flour, baking powder and salt. Add the apple, nuts and vanilla and mix well. Spoon into a greased baking dish. Bake at 350 degrees for 35 minutes. Serve with whipped cream or ice cream. Bake for 5 to 10 minutes longer if served as cookies. *Yield: 6 servings.*

Pat Squires

Party Cookies

1 cup butter, softened
½ cup confectioners' sugar
2 cups sifted flour

Beat the butter, confectioners' sugar and flour in a mixer bowl until blended, scraping the bowl occasionally. Press the dough through a cookie press onto an ungreased cookie sheet. Bake in a moderate oven until light brown. *Yield: 2 dozen cookies.*

Charlotte Sweeney Schmitt

Mrs. Irwin's Plain Cookies

1 1/2 cups flour	3/4 cup margarine or butter, softened	1 tablespoon vanilla extract
1/2 teaspoon baking powder	3/4 cup sugar	1/2 cup rolled oats
1/4 teaspoon salt	1 egg	1/2 cup Grape-Nuts cereal

Sift the flour, baking powder and salt into a bowl and mix well. Beat the margarine in a bowl until creamy. Add the sugar gradually, beating until light and fluffy. Beat in the egg and vanilla. Add the flour mixture and mix well. Stir in the oats and cereal. Shape into 1-inch balls. Arrange on a greased cookie sheet; flatten with a glass dipped in additional flour. Bake at 375 degrees for 10 minutes. May top cookies with sprinkles, chocolate chips or walnut halves before baking. *Yield: 3 dozen cookies.*

Carl Nold

Raisin Cookies

2 cups raisins	1 cup shortening	1 teaspoon cinnamon
1 cup water	3 eggs	1/2 teaspoon salt
1 teaspoon baking soda	1 teaspoon vanilla extract	1/4 teaspoon nutmeg
2 cups sugar	4 cups flour	1 cup chopped nuts
	1 teaspoon baking powder	

Combine the raisins and water in a saucepan. Bring to a boil. Boil for 5 minutes. Remove from heat. Stir in the baking soda. Let stand until cool. Beat the sugar, shortening and eggs in a mixer bowl until creamy. Stir in the raisin mixture and vanilla. Add the flour, baking powder, cinnamon, salt and nutmeg and mix well. Stir in the nuts. Drop by teaspoonfuls onto a buttered cookie sheet. Bake at 375 degrees until brown. Cool on the cookie sheet for 2 minutes. Remove to a wire rack to cool completely. *Yield: 4 dozen cookies.*

Doris Cooper

Russian Tea Cakes

1 cup butter, softened
1/2 cup sifted confectioners' sugar
1 teaspoon vanilla extract
2 1/4 cups sifted flour
1/4 teaspoon salt
3/4 cup finely chopped nuts
Confectioners' sugar to taste

Beat the butter, 1/2 cup confectioners' sugar and vanilla in a mixer bowl until smooth. Stir in a sifted mixture of the flour and salt. Add the nuts and mix well. Chill, covered, in the refrigerator. Shape into 1-inch balls. Arrange on an ungreased cookie sheet. Bake at 400 degrees for 10 to 12 minutes or until firm but not brown. Roll the warm cookies in confectioners' sugar to taste twice. *Yield: 2 dozen.*

Stella King

Sand Tarts

2/3 cup butter
1 cup sugar
2 eggs
1 tablespoon water
2 cups flour
1/2 teaspoon baking powder
Cinnamon and sugar to taste
1/4 cup almonds

Beat the butter in a mixer bowl until creamy. Add the sugar, beating until smooth. Beat in the eggs and water. Add a sifted mixture of the flour and baking powder, mixing until a stiff dough forms. Roll very thin on a lightly floured surface; cut into squares. Arrange on a non-stick cookie sheet. Sprinkle with cinnamon and sugar. Top each square with 2 to 3 almonds. Bake at 425 to 450 degrees for 6 to 10 minutes or until golden brown. *Yield: 2 dozen.*

Mrs. Vincent Switzer

Scotch Cookies

6 cups sifted flour
1 tablespoon baking soda
1/2 teaspoon salt
1 cup shortening

3 cups sugar
2 eggs, lightly beaten
1/2 cup molasses
1/4 cup water

2 teaspoons vanilla extract
1 egg
1 to 2 tablespoons milk

Sift the flour, baking soda and salt into a bowl and mix well. Beat the shortening in a mixer bowl until creamy. Add the sugar and 2 eggs. Beat until blended, scraping the bowl occasionally. Add the molasses, water and vanilla and mix well. Stir in the flour mixture. Roll 1/4 inch thick on a lightly floured surface; cut with a cookie cutter. Place on a nonstick cookie sheet. Brush with a mixture of 1 egg and milk. Bake at 375 degrees for 10 minutes. Cool on the cookie sheet for 2 minutes. Remove to a wire rack to cool completely. May substitute 1 1/2 cups margarine for the shortening and evaporated milk for the egg and milk mixture. Yield: 3 dozen cookies.

Joanne Zwolinski

Sour Cream Cookies

1/2 teaspoon baking soda
1/2 cup sour cream
1 1/2 cups sugar

1 cup shortening
2 eggs
1/2 teaspoon salt
1/2 teaspoon nutmeg

4 cups flour
Seeded raisins
Sugar to taste

Dissolve the baking soda in the sour cream and mix well. Beat 1 1/2 cups sugar, shortening, eggs, salt and nutmeg in a mixer bowl until creamy, scraping the bowl occasionally. Beat in the sour cream mixture. Stir in 3 cups of the flour and mix well. Sprinkle the remaining 1 cup flour on a hard surface. Knead the dough gently on the flour-coated surface until all of the flour has been incorporated into the dough. Roll the dough and cut with a large cookie cutter. Arrange on a nonstick cookie sheet. Place 1 or 2 raisins in the center of each cookie; sprinkle with sugar to taste. Bake at 350 degrees for 12 to 15 minutes or until light brown. Cool on the cookie sheet for 2 minutes. Remove to a wire rack to cool completely. Yield: 4 dozen cookies.

Florence Vance

Grandma Rodin's Spritz Cookies

1 cup butter, softened
1 cup sugar
2 eggs

2½ cups flour
1 teaspoon baking powder
1 teaspoon nutmeg

1 teaspoon extract of choice
Salt to taste

Beat the butter, sugar and eggs in a mixer bowl until creamy. Add the flour, baking powder, nutmeg, flavoring and salt and mix well. Chill, covered, for several minutes. Press the dough through a cookie press onto a nonstick cookie sheet. Bake at 450 degrees for 8 to 10 minutes. *Yield: 2 dozen cookies.*

Helga R. Doud

Sweetheart Cookies

¾ cup butter or margarine, softened
½ cup sugar

1 egg yolk
1½ cups flour
Raspberry jam

Confectioners' sugar to taste

Beat the butter, sugar and egg yolk in a mixer bowl until creamy, scraping the bowl occasionally. Add the flour and mix well. Chill, covered, for several hours. Shape into ¾-inch balls. Place on a greased cookie sheet. Make an indention in each ball with the back of a spoon or your thumb. Fill the indentions with jam. Bake at 375 degrees until light brown. Cool on the cookie sheet for 2 minutes. Remove to a wire rack to cool completely. Roll in confectioners' sugar. May substitute any flavor jam for the raspberry jam.
Yield: 2 dozen cookies.

Mrs. George Clark

Turtle Bars

2 cups flour
1 cup packed brown sugar
1/2 cup butter or margarine, softened

1 cup pecan halves
2/3 cup butter

1/2 cup packed brown sugar
1 to 2 cups milk chocolate chips

Combine the flour, 1 cup brown sugar and 1/2 cup butter in a mixer bowl. Beat at medium speed for 2 to 3 minutes or until blended, scraping the bowl frequently. Press into a 9x13-inch baking pan sprayed with nonstick cooking spray. Arrange the pecans over the prepared layer. Combine 2/3 cup butter and 1/2 cup brown sugar in a saucepan. Bring to a boil over medium heat, stirring constantly; reduce heat. Cook for 30 to 60 seconds, stirring constantly. Pour over the prepared layers. Bake at 350 degrees for 18 to 22 minutes or until the crust is golden brown. Sprinkle with the chocolate chips; cover loosely with foil. Let stand until the chocolate chips soften; spread with a knife. Let stand until cool. Cut into bars. Yield: 3 dozen bars.

Selma Dufina

Walnut Crescents

1/2 cup butter or margarine, softened
1/2 cup shortening
1/3 cup sugar

2 teaspoons water
2 teaspoons vanilla extract
2 cups flour

1/2 cup chopped black walnuts
Confectioners' sugar to taste

Beat the butter in a mixer bowl until creamy. Add the shortening and sugar, beating until light and fluffy. Add the water and vanilla and mix well. Beat in the flour. Stir in the walnuts. Chill, covered, for 3 to 4 hours. Shape the dough into 1/2-inch-thick ropes; cut into 3-inch lengths. Shape into crescents on an ungreased cookie sheet. Bake at 325 degrees for 15 minutes; do not brown. Cool slightly on a wire rack. Coat with confectioners' sugar. Yield: 4 dozen crescents.

Mary Truscott

Apple Crumb Pie

2/3 cup sugar
1 tablespoon butter, softened
3/4 teaspoon grated lemon peel
1/4 teaspoon salt
1/4 teaspoon cinnamon
1/4 teaspoon nutmeg
6 to 8 tart apples, chopped
1 unbaked (9-inch) pie shell
3/4 cup sifted flour
3/4 cup packed light brown sugar
1/4 cup sugar
1/4 teaspoon salt
1/2 cup margarine, softened

Combine 2/3 cup sugar, butter, lemon peel, 1/4 teaspoon salt, cinnamon and nutmeg in a bowl and mix well. Add the apples, tossing to mix. Spoon into the pie shell. Combine the flour, brown sugar, 1/4 cup sugar and 1/4 teaspoon salt in a bowl and mix well. Cut in the margarine until crumbly. Sprinkle over the prepared layer. Bake at 375 degrees until bubbly and brown. *Yield: 6 servings.*

Meg Brown

Buttermilk Pie

1 cup sugar
3 tablespoons flour
1/2 teaspoon salt
2 cups buttermilk
3 egg yolks, lightly beaten
1/4 cup melted butter or margarine, cooled
3 egg whites
1/4 teaspoon cream of tartar
1 unbaked (9-inch) pie shell

Combine the sugar, flour and salt in a bowl and mix well. Combine the buttermilk, egg yolks and butter in a bowl and mix well. Add to the flour mixture gradually, beating well after each addition. Beat the egg whites in a mixer bowl until foamy. Add the cream of tartar. Beat until stiff peaks form. Fold into the buttermilk mixture. Spoon into the pie shell. Bake at 375 degrees for 45 minutes. *Yield: 6 servings.*

Agnes Shine

Banana Butterscotch Pie

1 cup sugar
2 tablespoons flour
1 tablespoon (rounded) butter
2 egg yolks
1 cup cold water
1 teaspoon vanilla extract
1 large banana, sliced
1 baked (9-inch) pie shell
2 egg whites
1/4 cup sugar

Combine 1 cup sugar, flour, butter and egg yolks in a saucepan, stirring until a smooth paste forms. Stir in the cold water. Cook until thickened, stirring constantly. Remove from heat. Stir in the vanilla. Arrange the banana slices over the bottom of the pie shell. Spoon the custard over the banana. Beat the egg whites in a mixer bowl until foamy. Add 1/4 cup sugar gradually, beating constantly until stiff peaks form. Spread over the filling, sealing to the edge. Bake at 400 degrees for 8 minutes or until brown. *Yield: 6 servings.*

Joanne Zwolinski

Butterscotch Pie

3/4 cup packed brown sugar
1/3 cup flour
1/4 cup sugar
2 cups milk, scalded
1/8 teaspoon salt
3 egg yolks, beaten
1 1/2 tablespoons butter
1 teaspoon vanilla extract
1 baked (9-inch) pie shell
3 egg whites
6 tablespoons sugar

Combine the brown sugar, flour and 1/4 cup sugar in a double boiler and mix well. Add the hot milk gradually, stirring constantly until blended. Stir in the salt. Cook for 15 minutes or until thickened, stirring constantly. Stir a small amount of the hot mixture into the egg yolks; stir the egg yolks into the hot mixture. Cook for 3 minutes, stirring constantly. Add the butter, stirring until melted. Let stand until cool. Stir in the vanilla. Spoon into the pie shell. Beat the egg whites in a mixer bowl until foamy. Add 6 tablespoons sugar gradually, beating constantly until stiff peaks form. Spread over the filling, sealing to the edge. Bake at 325 degrees for 15 to 18 minutes or until brown. *Yield: 6 servings.*

June Brown

French Silk Chocolate Pie

3/4 cup sugar
1/2 cup butter or margarine, softened
2 ounces chocolate, melted
1 teaspoon vanilla extract
2 eggs
1 baked (9-inch) pie shell or graham cracker pie shell

Beat the sugar and butter in a mixer bowl until creamy. Add the chocolate and vanilla and mix well. Add the eggs 1 at a time, beating for 5 minutes after each addition. Spoon into the pie shell. Chill, covered, overnight. Serve plain or with a dollop of whipped topping or whipped cream. To avoid raw eggs that may carry salmonella we suggest using an equivalent amount of commercial egg substitute. *Yield: 6 servings.*

Caroline LaPine

Cottage Cheese Pie

1 cup cottage cheese
1/2 cup sugar
1 tablespoon flour
1 egg white
1 egg
1 egg yolk
1/2 cup half-and-half
1/2 cup sugar
Vanilla extract to taste
Cinnamon to taste

Mix the cottage cheese, 1/2 cup sugar, flour and egg white in a bowl. Pat into a pie plate. Beat the egg and egg yolk in a mixer bowl until foamy. Add the half-and-half, 1/2 cup sugar and vanilla, beating until blended. Spoon into the prepared pie plate. Sprinkle with cinnamon. Bake at 350 degrees for 30 to 40 minutes or until set. *Yield: 6 servings.*

Joanne Zwolinski

Cran-Raspberry Pie

2 cups sugar
1/4 cup tapioca
1 teaspoon almond extract
12 ounces fresh cranberries
2 cups raspberries
1 recipe (2-crust) pie pastry

Mix the sugar, tapioca and flavoring in a bowl. Stir in the cranberries and raspberries. Spoon into a pastry-lined pie plate. Cut the remaining pastry into strips; arrange lattice-fashion over the pie. Bake at 375 degrees for 45 minutes. *Yield: 6 servings.*

Meg Brown

Lemon Meringue Pie

2 cups boiling water
1 1/2 cups sugar
1/2 cup cornstarch

Grated peel of 1 lemon
Juice of 2 lemons
3 egg yolks, lightly beaten
1/4 teaspoon salt

1 baked (9-inch) pie shell
3 egg whites
6 tablespoons sugar

Combine the boiling water and 1 1/2 cups sugar in a double boiler, stirring until the sugar dissolves. Add the cornstarch and mix well. Stir in a mixture of the lemon peel and lemon juice. Add the egg yolks and salt and mix well. Cook until thickened, stirring constantly. Spoon into the pie shell. Beat the egg whites in a mixer bowl until foamy. Add 6 tablespoons sugar gradually, beating constantly until stiff peaks form. Spread over the filling, sealing to the edges. Bake until light brown. *Yield: 6 servings.*

Mattie Blanchard

Murray Special Pecan Pie

1 cup pecan pieces
1 unbaked (9-inch) pie shell

3 eggs
1 cup dark corn syrup
3/4 cup sugar
1/4 cup melted butter

1/4 cup coffee cream
1/8 teaspoon salt
(optional)

Sprinkle 1/2 cup of the pecans over the bottom of the pie shell. Beat the eggs lightly in a mixer bowl. Add the corn syrup, sugar, butter and cream gradually, beating until blended. Stir in the salt. Spoon into the prepared pie shell. Sprinkle with the remaining 1/2 cup pecans. Bake at 350 degrees for 40 minutes or until almost set. Reduce the oven temperature to 225 degrees. Bake for 15 minutes longer or until set. *Yield: 6 servings.*

Ethel Ross, Murray Hotel

Rum Pecan Pie

1 cup light corn syrup
2/3 cup sugar
1/4 cup melted butter or margarine
1/4 cup light rum
1 teaspoon vanilla extract
3 eggs
1 cup chopped pecans
1 unbaked (9-inch) pie shell
20 whole pecans

Beat the corn syrup, sugar, butter, rum, vanilla and eggs in a mixer bowl for 3 to 4 minutes. Fold in the chopped pecans. Spoon into the pie shell. Arrange the whole pecans in a circle around the outer edge of the filling. Bake at 375 degrees for 45 minutes. Remove to a wire rack to cool completely. Garnish with whipped cream. *Yield: 6 servings.*

Lornie Porter

Rhubarb Pie

1 cup sugar
3 tablespoons flour
1/8 teaspoon salt
1/2 teaspoon grated orange peel
3 cups chopped rhubarb
1 recipe (2-crust) pie pastry
2 tablespoons butter

Combine the sugar, flour, salt and orange peel in a bowl and mix well. Add the rhubarb, tossing to mix. Spoon into a pastry-lined pie plate. Dot with the butter. Top with the remaining pastry, sealing the edge and cutting vents. Bake at 450 degrees for 10 minutes. Reduce the oven temperature to 350 degrees. Bake for 30 minutes longer. *Yield: 6 servings.*

Joanne Zwolinski

Fresh Strawberry Pie

3 cups whole strawberries	1 cup crushed strawberries	1 1/2 tablespoons cornstarch
1/2 cup confectioners' sugar	1 cup water	1 baked (9-inch) pie shell
	1/2 to 3/4 cup sugar	

Combine 3 cups whole strawberries with confectioners' sugar in a bowl, tossing to coat. Let stand for 1 hour. Combine 1 cup crushed strawberries and water in a saucepan. Cook for 2 minutes, stirring frequently. May strain if desired. Stir in a mixture of the sugar and cornstarch. Cook until clear, stirring constantly. Arrange the whole strawberries in the pie shell. Pour the hot strawberry mixture over the strawberries. Let stand until cool. Garnish each serving with whipped cream. *Yield: 6 servings.*

Mrs. Lowell Johnston

Best-Ever Pie Pastries

3 cups sifted flour	1 cup shortening	1 tablespoon vinegar
1 teaspoon salt	1/3 cup cold water	1 egg, beaten

Sift the flour and salt into a bowl and mix well. Cut in the shortening until crumbly. Stir in a mixture of the cold water, vinegar and egg. Stir gently with a fork until the dough adheres. Shape into a ball. Chill, covered for 1 to 2 hours. May substitute a mixture of 1/2 cup butter and 1/2 cup shortening or lard for 1 cup shortening. *Yield: 2 (2-crust) pie pastries.*

Marie Newell

Index

APPETIZERS
Asparagus Roll-Ups, 26
Boursin Cheese, 20
Broccoli and Cheese Skins, 26
Cheese Ball, 20
Cheese Fingers, 28
Dill Dip, 22
Ham Rolls, 27
Herb Cheese Spread, 21
Hot Cheese Dip, 21
Hot Nacho Dip, 23
Liptauer Spread, 24
Liver Sausage Spread, 25
Party Mix, 28
Romanola, 29
Salmon Log, 25
Skinny Dipping, 23
Taco Dip, 24
Triple Cheese Dip, 22

APPLE
Apple Cake, 128
Apple Crisp, 116
Apple Crumb Pie, 164
Apple Crumb Pie Dessert, 116
Apple Mallow Yam Bake, 81
Five-Cup Salad, 35
Fruit and Nut Bread Pudding, 121
Ozark Cookies, 158
Waldorf Salad, 38

APRICOT
Apricot Bread, 92
Apricot Fluff, 34
Fruit Squares, 154

ASPARAGUS
Asparagus and Tomato Casserole, 17
Asparagus Casserole, 74
Asparagus Roll-Ups, 26

BANANA
Banana Butterscotch Pie, 165
Banana Cake, 129
Banana Frosting, 130
Banana Luncheon Bread, 93
Banana Sheet Cake, 130
Black Walnut Banana Cake, 129
Ray's Banana Bread, 93

BEANS
Bean Soup, 30
Bob-Lo Barbecue Bean Bake, 48
Marinated Bean Salad, 40
String Bean Salad, 40
Sweet Baked Beans, 75

BEEF. *See also* Ground Beef
Italian Beef Steaks, 46
Lazy-Day Beef Casserole, 47
Lemon Pepper Roast, 46
Pot Roast, 46
Sukiyaki, 47

BEVERAGES
Frozen Daiquiris, 29
Mackinac Frozen Margaritas, 29

BISCUITS
Cheese Biscuits, 88
Neapolitan or Buttermilk Biscuits, 88

BRAN
Bran Bread, 94
Bran Muffins, 99

BREADS. *See also* Biscuits; Coffee Cakes; Muffins; Rolls
Cinnamon Sticks, 112
Cinnamon Twists, 111
Doughnuts, 113
For-Sure Popovers, 113
French Croissants, 106
Pecan Twists, 110
Rosettes, 114
Scottish Scones, 89
Southern Spoon Bread, 91
Sticky Hot Cross Buns, 109
Ukranian Kolache, 112
Yorkshire Pudding, 114

BREADS, LOAVES
Apricot Bread, 92
Banana Luncheon Bread, 93
Bran Bread, 94
Cinnamon Bread, 95
Coffee-Can Bread, 101
Cranberry Bread, 95
Date-Nut Bread, 96
Dilly Bread, 102
Egg Bread, 102
French Bread I, 103
French Bread II, 103
Irish Brown Bread, 94
Julekage, 104
Nut Bread, 96
Oatmeal Bread, 104
Orange Bread, 97
Orange Quick Bread, 97
Prune Bread, 98
Pumpkin Bread, 98
Ray's Banana Bread, 93
Swedish Rye Bread, 105
White Bread, 105
Zucchini Bread, 99

BROCCOLI
Broccoli and Cheese Skins, 26
Broccoli Bacon Salad, 41
Broccoli Stuffing Casserole, 76

BROWNIES
Brownies, 152
Rocky Road Brownies, 153

CAKES
Apple Cake, 128
Banana Cake, 129
Banana Sheet Cake, 130
Black Walnut Banana Cake, 129
Blueberry Cake, 131
Butter Sponge Cake, 146

Carrot Cake, 132
Chocolate Chip Date Cake, 132
Chocolate Pastry Cakes, 135
Chop Suey Cake, 137
Company Cake, 133
Coronation Cake, 134
Craters-of-the-Moon Cake, 137
Cream-Coated Devil's Food
  Cake, 134
Fruitcakes, 138
Grandma Libby's Pumpkin
  Cake, 144
Hawaiian Cake, 140
Large Chocolate Sour Cream
  Sheet Cake, 135
Mackinac Sailing Cake, 141
Mayonnaise Cake, 141
Mississippi Mud Cake, 142
Old-Fashioned Jelly Roll, 140
Orange Cake, 143
Pineapple Torte, 145
Poppy Seed Cake, 143
Rhubarb Cake, 144
Sock-It-To-Me Cake, 145
St. Fanny Cake, 136
Very Best Fruitcakes, 139
Yeast Chocolate Cake, 136
Yuletide Cake, 147

CANDY
Divinity, 125
Easy No-Bake Cookies, 126
English Toffee, 128
Million-Dollar Fudge, 126
Peanut Butter Bars, 128
Superior Fudge, 127
Won't Fail Fudge, 127

CARROT
Carrot Cake, 132
Carrot Soufflé, 76
Spiced Carrots, 77

CHEESECAKE
Cheesecake, 118
Pineapple Cheesecake, 117

CHICKEN
Chalupas, 63
Chicken Casserole, 67
Chicken Della Robbia, 64
Chicken Parmesan, 65
Chinese Walnut Chicken, 66
Easy Popover Chicken, 65
French-Canadian Meat Pie, 55
Golfers' Chicken, 64
Hot Chicken Salad, 39
Party Chicken, 16
Stir-Fried Chicken, 66
Sweet-and-Sour Chicken, 67

CHOCOLATE. *See also* Fudge
Cherries and Chocolate, 117
Chocolate Chip Biscotti, 151
Chocolate Chip Date
  Cake, 132
Chocolate Fondue, 125
Chocolate Frosting, 152
Chocolate Glaze, 119, 153
Chocolate Icing, 135
Chocolate Pastry Cakes, 135
Chocolate Squares, 151
Cran-Raspberry Pie, 166
Craters-of-the Moon Cake, 137
Cream-Coated Devil's Food
  Cake, 134
Delightful Cookies, 153
French Silk Chocolate Pie, 166
Irish Cookies, 155
Large Chocolate Sour Cream
  Sheet Cake, 135
Mayonnaise Cake, 141
Mississippi Mud Cake, 142
Mississippi Mud Frosting, 142
Turtle Bars, 163
Yeast Chocolate Cake, 136

COFFEE CAKES
Aunt Leila's Coffee Cakes, 89
Easy Coffee Cake, 90
Frozen Biscuit Coffee
  Cake, 90
Vienna Coffee Cake, 91

COOKIES
Aggression Cookies, 150
Angel Cookies, 150
Bourbon Balls, 152
Brownies, 152
Cheesecake Cookies, 18
Chocolate Chip Biscotti, 151
Chocolate Squares, 151
Delightful Cookies, 153
Fruit Squares, 154
Galettes or French Cakes, 155
Grandma Rodin's Spritz
  Cookies, 162
Irish Cookies, 155
Lemon Squares, 156
Lizzies, 156
Mincemeat Hermits, 157
Mrs. Irwin's Plain Cookies, 159
Oatmeal Refrigerator
  Cookies, 158
Old-Fashioned Ginger
  Cookies, 154
Ozark Cookies, 158
Party Cookies, 158
Peanut Butter Oatmeal
  Cookies, 157
Raisin Cookies, 159
Rocky Road Brownies, 153
Russian Tea Cakes, 160
Sand Tarts, 160
Scotch Cookies, 161
Sour Cream Cookies, 161
Sweetheart Cookies, 162
Turtle Bars, 163
Walnut Crescents, 163

CRAB MEAT
Crab Bisque, 33
Crab Meat Delight, 72

CRANBERRY
Chili and Cranberry Sauce, 51
Congealed Cranberry
  Salad, 34
Cran-Raspberry Pie, 166
Cranberry Bread, 95

171

Frozen Cranberry Salad, 35

DESSERTS. *See also* Cakes; Candy; Cheesecake; Cookies; Fruitcakes; Ice Cream; Pies; Puddings
  Apple Crisp, 116
  Apple Crumb Pie Dessert, 116
  Cherries and Chocolate, 117
  Chocolate Fondue, 125
  Cream Cheese Dessert, 118
  Cream Puffs, 119
  Mackinac Plum Crunch, 124
  Prune Whip, 124
  So-Easy Cream Puffs, 120

DESSERTS, SAUCES
  Fudge Sauce, 125
  Hard Sauce, 122
  Hard Sauce for Blueberry Cake, 131

DIPS
  Dill Dip, 22
  Hot Cheese Dip, 21
  Hot Nacho Dip, 23
  Skinny Dipping, 23
  Taco Dip, 24
  Triple Cheese Dip, 22

EGGPLANT
  Eggplant Parmigiana, 77
  Italian Vegetable Casserole, 60

ENCHILADAS
  Cheese Enchiladas, 15

FILLINGS
  Creamy Citrus Filling, 36
  Custard Filling, 133, 143
  Lemon Filling, 146
  Vanilla Filling, 119

FISH. *See also* Salmon
  Baked Stuffed Whitefish, 69
  Baked Whitefish Fillets, 68
  Boiled Whitefish, 69
  Capilotade of Fish, 68
  Fish Chowder, 33
  Mackinac Whitefish with Wine Sauce, 70

FROSTINGS/ICINGS
  Aunt Nonie's Frosting, 149
  Banana Frosting, 130
  Busy-Day Icing, 147
  Butter Frosting, 144
  Chocolate Frosting, 152
  Chocolate Glaze, 119, 153
  Chocolate Icing, 135
  Coconut Icing, 134
  Confectioners' Sugar Icing, 109
  Cream Cheese Frosting, 137
  Creamy Nut Frosting, 148
  Fluffy Uncooked Frosting, 149
  Lemon Butter Icing, 148
  Marshmallow Frosting, 146
  Mississippi Mud Frosting, 142
  Quick Icing, 148
  Swirl Frosting, 149
  Vanilla Frosting, 140

FRUITCAKES
  Fruitcakes, 138
  Very Best Fruitcakes, 139

FUDGE
  Fudge Sauce, 125
  Million-Dollar Fudge, 126
  Superior Fudge, 127
  Won't Fail Fudge, 127

GROUND BEEF
  Bob-Lo Barbecue Bean Bake, 48
  Cheesy Ground Beef Casserole, 49
  Ground Beef Goulash, 49
  Ground Beef Stroganoff, 50
  Meatballs, 51
  Meat Pasties, 53
  Meat Pie, 53
  My Mother's Chili, 48
  Norwegian Meatballs, 52
  Open-Faced Hamburgers, 51
  Scotch Meat Pie, 54
  Spaghetti, 50
  Swedish Meatballs, 52

HAM
  Ham Loaf, 58
  Ham Rolls, 27
  Scalloped Ham and Egg Casserole, 58

HORS D'OEUVRE
  Asparagus Roll-Ups, 26
  Broccoli and Cheese Skins, 26
  Cheese Fingers, 28
  Ham Rolls, 27

ICE CREAM
  Six Threes Ice Cream, 121

LAMB
  Quick Lamb Curry, 56

LEMON
  Lemon Butter Icing, 148
  Lemon Filling, 146
  Lemon Meringue Pie, 167
  Lemon Squares, 156

MEATBALLS
  Meatballs, 51
  Norwegian Meatballs, 52
  Swedish Meatballs, 52

MUFFINS
  Bran Muffins, 99
  Float-Away Tea Cake Muffins, 100
  Poppy Seed Muffins, 101
  Raised Cornmeal Muffins, 92
  Zucchini Muffins, 100

ORANGE
  Creamy Citrus Filling, 36

Five-Cup Salad, 35
Mandarin Orange Salad, 36
Orange Bread, 97
Orange Cake, 143
Orange Quick Bread, 97

PASTRY
Best-Ever Pie Pastries, 169
French-Canadian Meat Pie
    Pastry, 55
Scotch Meat Pie Pastry, 54

PEANUT BUTTER
Peanut Butter Bars, 128
Peanut Butter Oatmeal
    Cookies, 157

PECAN
Murray Special Pecan Pie, 167
Rum Pecan Pie, 168

PIES
Apple Crumb Pie, 164
Banana Butterscotch Pie, 165
Buttermilk Pie, 164
Butterscotch Pie, 165
Cottage Cheese Pie, 166
Cran-Raspberry Pie, 166
French Silk Chocolate Pie, 166
Fresh Strawberry Pie, 169
Lemon Meringue Pie, 167
Murray Special Pecan Pie, 167
Rhubarb Pie, 168
Rum Pecan Pie, 168
Surprise Walnut Pie, 18

PIES, MEAT
French-Canadian Meat Pie, 55
Meat Pasties, 53
Meat Pie, 53
Scotch Meat Pie, 54
Venison Pie, 63

PINEAPPLE
Creamy Citrus Filling, 36
Hawaiian Cake, 140

Pineapple Cheesecake, 117
Pineapple Torte, 145
Watergate Salad, 38

PIZZA
Bubble-Up Pizza, 61

PORK. *See also* Ham; Sausage
Barbecued Spareribs, 57
French-Canadian Meat Pie, 55
Smothered Potatoes, 56
Swedish Meatballs, 52

POTATO
Carriage House Special
    German Potato Soup, 32
Company Potatoes, 78
Deep-Fried Potato Balls, 79
Hot German Potato Salad, 79
Potatoes Deluxe, 78
Potato Pancakes, 80
Smothered Potatoes, 56
Stampede Potato Pudding, 80
Venison Steak with Stout and
    Potatoes, 62

PRUNES
Fruit Squares, 154
Prune Bread, 98
Prune Whip, 124

PUDDINGS
English Plum Pudding, 122
Fruit and Nut Bread
    Pudding, 121
Lemon Sponge Pudding, 123
Slip Custard, 120
Voletta Cherry Pudding, 123

PUMPKIN
Grandma Libby's Pumpkin
    Cake, 144
Pumpkin Bread, 98

RASPBERRY
Cran-Raspberry Pie, 166

Raspberry Salad, 37
Sweetheart Cookies, 162

RHUBARB
Rhubarb Cake, 144
Rhubarb Pie, 168

ROLLS
Aunt Jessie's Old Southern
    Buttermilk Rolls, 106
Famous Rolls, 107
Feather Bed Rolls, 107
Refrigerator Rolls, 108

SALADS, DRESSINGS
Celery Seed Salad Dressing, 43
Creamy Salad Dressing, 43
Green Goddess Salad
    Dressing, 44
Honey Dressing for Fruit
    Salad, 44
Roquefort Dressing, 44
Spinach Salad Dressing, 41

SALADS, FRUIT
Apricot Fluff, 34
Congealed Cranberry Salad, 34
Five-Cup Salad, 35
Frozen Cranberry Salad, 35
Lime Cream Cheese Salad, 36
Mandarin Orange Salad, 36
Raspberry Salad, 37
Strawberry Sour Cream Gelatin
    Mold, 37
Waldorf Salad, 38
Watergate Salad, 38

SALADS, MAIN DISH
Hot Chicken Salad, 39
Shrimp Salad, 39

SALADS, VEGETABLE
Broccoli Bacon Salad, 41
Hot German Potato Salad, 79
Italian Tomato Salad, 42
Marinated Bean Salad, 40

173

Spinach Salad, 41
String Bean Salad, 40
Tomato Aspic Salad, 42
Wonderful Vegetable
  Salad, 43

SALMON
Salmon and Vegetables, 71
Salmon Loaf, 71
Salmon Log, 25

SAUCES
Barbecue Sauce, 85
Chili and Cranberry Sauce, 51
Fresh Tomato Sauce, 86
Mushroom Sauce, 65
Sweet-and-Sour Sauce, 85
Tomato Sauce, 86
Wine Sauce, 70

SAUSAGE
Breakfast Surprise, 59
Bubble-Up Pizza, 61
Coddle, 60
Italian Vegetable Casserole, 60
Lasagna, 61
Liver Sausage Spread, 25
Sausage Ball-Stuffed Squash, 81
Spaghetti Sauce with Italian
  Sausage, 62
Surprise Soufflé, 59

SEAFOOD. *See also* Crab Meat;
  Shrimp
Seafood Quiche, 74

SHRIMP
Curry of Shrimp, 73
Shrimp Casserole Harpin, 72

Shrimp Creole, 72
Shrimp Salad, 39

SIDE DISHES
Baked Noodle Casserole, 83
Conserve for Meat, 84
Gleasants, 84
Rice and Cheese Soufflé, 83

SNACKS
Party Mix, 28
Romanola, 29

SOUPS
Bean Soup, 30
Carriage House Special
  German Potato Soup, 32
Cheesy Vegetable Soup, 32
Corn Chowder, 31
Crab Bisque, 33
Cucumber Soup, 30
Fish Chowder, 33
French Canadian Pea
  Soup, 31

SPINACH
Spinach and Cheese Tart, 80
Spinach Salad, 41

SPREADS
Boursin Cheese, 20
Cheese Ball, 20
Herb Cheese Spread, 21
Liptauer Spread, 24
Liver Sausage Spread, 25
Salmon Log, 25

STRAWBERRY
Fresh Strawberry Pie, 169

Strawberry Sour Cream Gelatin
  Mold, 37

TOMATO
Asparagus and Tomato
  Casserole, 17
Fresh Tomato Sauce, 86
Italian Tomato Salad, 42
Tomato Aspic Salad, 42
Tomato Sauce, 86

VEGETABLES. *See also* Individual
  Kinds; Salads, Vegetable
Apple Mallow Yam Bake, 81
Cheesy Vegetable Soup, 32
Grandma's Harvard Beets, 75
Italian Vegetable Casserole, 60
Sausage Ball-Stuffed Squash, 81
Vegetables au Gratin, 82

VENISON
Venison Pie, 63
Venison Steak with Stout and
  Potatoes, 62

WALNUT
Black Walnut Banana
  Cake, 129
Chinese Walnut Chicken, 66
Surprise Walnut Pie, 18
Walnut Crescents, 163
Zucchini with Walnuts, 82

Yorkshire Pudding, 114

ZUCCHINI
Zucchini Bread, 99
Zucchini Muffins, 100
Zucchini with Walnuts, 82

Order Information

The Flavors of Mackinac
Mackinac Island Medical Center
P.O. Box 536 · Market Street
Mackinac Island, Michigan 49757
(906) 847-3582

Please send _____ copies of *The Flavors of Mackinac* @ $18.00 each $ _____

Shipping and handling @ $ 3.50 each $ _____

Total $ _____

Name:
Address:
City: State: Zip:

Make checks or money oders payable to Mackinac Island Medical Center

The proceeds from the sale of this book support the Mackinac Island Medical Center.